THE LAST HENDON FARM

The archaeology and history of Church End Farm

Copyright © Hendon and District Archaeological Society

All rights reserved. No part of this publication may be reproduced, stored in a retrieval system or transmitted in any form or by any means, electronic, mechanical, photocopying, recording or otherwise without the prior permission of the copyright owner.

Production by Tracy Wellman, Museum of London Archaeology Service
Typesetting and design by Sue Cawood
Printed by the Trafford Press
ISBN 0 9503050

Front cover: detail from Cook's map of 1796 showing Church End, Hendon (reproduced by permission of LBBLSA)

THE LAST HENDON FARM

The archaeology and history of Church End Farm

by
Stephen Brunning, Don Cooper, Elizabeth Gapp, Geraldine Missig, Tim Nicholson
and Christopher Willey

Edited by Jacqui Pearce (Museum of London Specialist Services)

DEDICATED TO THE MEMORY OF TED SAMMES AND IAN ROBERTSON

The last Hendon farm
CONTENTS

FOREWORD vii
ACKNOWLEDGEMENTS viii

■ CHAPTER 1: BEGINNINGS AND DISCOVERIES 1

How it all began 1
The first HADAS excavation 2
    Unscrambling the archive 3
    The Farmhouse (Site 1) 4
    The Paddock (Site 2) 6
    The Barn (Site 3) 7
    Looking back over the excavation records 8

■ CHAPTER 2: SETTING THE SCENE 9

The location of the sites 9
The lie of the land 10
What kind of farm? 10
The historical context 11

■ CHAPTER 3: THE FARM AND ITS OCCUPANTS 13

Farmer, husbandman and bricklayer 13
Land use in the 18th and 19th centuries 18
Earlier 19th-century land use and historical context 19
William Sweetland, dairyman 20
The Model Dairy Farm 21
The Hinge family 22

CHAPTER 4: THE FARMSTEAD AND ITS BUILDINGS ... 25

The farmhouse: standing remains and photographs (Site 1) ... 25
The farmhouse in its national and regional context ... 25
An approximation of the building history ... 26
    PHASE 1: 1625–1660 ... 27
    PHASE 2: 1660-1760 ... 30
    PHASE 3: 1760-1785 ... 33
    PHASE 4: 1785-1810 ... 34
    PHASE 5: 1810-1860 ... 36
    PHASE 6: 1860 – demolition ... 37
The Barn (Site 3) as a standing building ... 38

CHAPTER 5: THE THINGS OF EVERYDAY LIFE ... 42

The earliest finds: from Roman to Tudor ... 42
The pottery ... 42
    Broad chronological trends ... 43
    Everyday household crocks for the kitchen and storeroom ... 44
    Dining in style ... 47
    Hot and cold beverages of every kind ... 52
    Health, hygiene and other household needs ... 55
    Stonewares from the Rhineland ... 55
    Bird pots and sparrow pie ... 57
A good pipe of tobacco ... 61
    Early pipes – the 17th century ... 61
    A longer smoke – pipes in the 18th century ... 63
    Victorian fancies ... 64
Wine bottles, phials and window glass ... 65
Bricks and tiles: the fabric of the building ... 68
    Late medieval floor tiles ... 68
    Tin-glazed wall and floor tiles ... 69
    Victorian tiles ... 70
Coins and tokens ... 71
An ivory comb, toys, tools and knives ... 73

Animal bones: daily food and wildlife 74
    Historical background 75
    The bones 75
    The species 76
    Condition of the bones 76
    The other species 78
    Conclusion 80

■ CHAPTER 6: FUTURE WORK 81

■ APPENDIX 1: DOCUMENTARY SOURCES FOR CHURCH END FARM FARMHOUSE AND FARM 82

Primary sources 82
Secondary sources 82
Mapping 82
    Crow's map, 1754 83
    Catalogue of Sale for the Parish Lands of Hendon 1754/6, mapping 83
    Messeder's 'A plan of the Manor & Parish of Hendon, 1783' ~ a copy of the 1754 original ... 83
    Rankin and Johnson's estate plan for Church End Farm 'estate' surveyed by J Prickett, 1789 83
    Cook's Map 1796, with associated Field Book 83
    Walter Johnson's estate maps 83
    OS sequence, 25 inches to 1 mile (latterly 1:2500), editions of 1863, 1914, 1936 and 1956, for Hendon village 84

■ APPENDIX 2: CHRONOLOGICAL LIST OF PROBABLE OCCUPANTS OF CHURCH END FARM, 1741 TO 1940 84

■ BIBLIOGRAPHY & END NOTES 86

The last Hendon farm
ACKNOWLEDGEMENTS

This book would not have been possible without a considerable amount of hard work and enthusiasm on the part of members of the post-diploma course in post-excavation analysis and publication, Faculty of Continuing Education, Birkbeck College, University of London. If it had not been for the inspiration and guidance of Andrew Selkirk and Harvey Sheldon, the course would never have happened, and to them we owe a special debt of gratitude. Continued help and advice has been provided on behalf of Birkbeck by Louise Rayner. Over the course of four years, many individuals have been involved in the project and have contributed to the present publication in any number of ways: Andrew Coulson, Laura Ellis, Ian Herbertson, Jill Hooper, Fay Stevens and Margaret White. We are very grateful to those members of the Museum of London Specialist Services (MoLSS) and others who have provided insights into the archaeology and history of Church End Farm: Geoff Egan, Jane Liddle, Jackie Keilly and Alan Pipe. In the context of the building record report special thanks are given to Terry Smith and Ian Betts, both of MoLSS, for their advice on the general context of the site, on elements of the photographic and map record, and on some of the surviving finds. We would also like to thank John Shepherd, formerly of the London Archaeological Archive and Research Centre, for helpful comments on the glass; Miranda Goodby, Collections Officer at The Potteries Museum and Art Gallery, Stoke-on-Trent for information on the Victorian floor tiles; and Kim Stabler, of English Heritage, for advice on site stratigraphy. Invaluable advice on the recording and identification of animal bones was provided by Professor Tony Legge, formerly of Birkbeck College. Thanks are also expressed to staff past and present at the London Borough of Barnet Local Studies and Archive Centre, including Andrew Mussel, Hugh Petrie and Yasmine Webb, and to Gerrard Roots, Curator of Church Farmhouse Museum, London Borough of Barnet. Especial thanks are extended to Tim Nicholson, architect and building conservator, for his work on the 'reconstruction' of Church End farmhouse from its photographic and other memorials. We are also extremely grateful to Clive and David Smith, of Memories, Brent Street, Hendon for copying photographs for publication and for kind permission to use the image reproduced in Fig 31, as well as for much helpful information on Church End Farm.

Figures 9, 11, 12, 14, 15, 18, 19 and 27 are reproduced by kind permission of LBBLSA, and Fig 4 courtesy of Simmons Aerofilms. Figure 16 is published here with permission of Alan Godfrey Ltd and of the Controller of Her Majesty's Stationery Office © Crown Copyright NC/05/40531). The images reproduced in Figs 49 and 51 are copyright Museum of London. The print illustrated in Fig 53 is published by courtesy of the Hogarth House Museum, Chiswick; the help of Andrea Cameron is gratefully acknowledged.

Tracy Wellman, of the Museum of London Archaeology Service, advised on design and production and this book has benefited greatly from her considerable expertise.

The last Hendon farm
FOREWORD

Denis Ross, Hon Secretary, Hendon and District Archaeological Society

I joined the Birkbeck course on 'Post-excavation analysis of materials from the Sammes archive' in its second year, starting in September 2002. I did so for a number of reasons. First, my interest in archaeology generally goes back a long time and I have attended a good many previous Birkbeck courses. Secondly, as Secretary of HADAS I thought I ought to know what the course was all about and what was going on. Thirdly, although my membership of HADAS did not overlap to any substantial extent the involvement of Ted Sammes, he holds a prestigious position in the memory of HADAS and I was interested in knowing something of what he had been up to. On joining the course, I made it clear that I did so mainly as an observer rather than a detailed participant. I am very glad I did join. I greatly enjoyed (although humbled by) the enormous expertise of the specialists who led the course. In addition, I admired the dedication in their respective fields of the other participants on the course and their contributions to this report. I believe their work has resulted in a publication of a high standard and considerable interest, which honours the memory of Ted Sammes and is a precursor to further reports on his activities in the Hendon area.

The last Hendon farm
CHAPTER 1:

BEGINNINGS AND DISCOVERIES

■ How it all began

Jacqui Pearce

In 1961 HADAS burst into life with a full-scale archaeological excavation! The express aim of the new-born Hendon and District Archaeological Society and its founder, Themistocles Constantinides, was to discover the Anglo-Saxon origins of Hendon. The catalyst was the imminent demolition of buildings at Hinge's Yard, the site of Church End Farm, situated in a prime position opposite the parish church of Hendon St Mary, at the top of what is now Greyhound Hill. If evidence for the Saxons was to be found, this seemed the ideal place to look, close to the church and the early post-Roman focus of settlement in Hendon. As it turned out, the society's first excavation was a great success in terms of the archaeology, but no sign of any Anglo-Saxon presence was uncovered. This had to wait another ten years or so, when a site on the opposite side of the road and close by the church began to yield sherds of Saxon chaff-tempered pottery and other finds.

In September 2001, HADAS embarked on an ambitious and exciting project in collaboration with the Faculty of Continuing Education, Birkbeck College, University of London and professional archaeologists from the Museum of London. A series of evening classes was set up at Avenue House, Finchley, and, by the time of publication, has been running successfully for four years. The aim of the course has been to revisit these early excavations carried out by HADAS in Hendon in the 1960s and '70s, to bring the site archives up to current standards and to publish the results, providing hands-on experience and training for course members in modern post-excavation methods and procedures.

Excavations on the site of Church End Farm, Hendon from 1961 to 1966, and at nearby Church Terrace in the 1970s uncovered a considerable quantity of finds, and generated much local interest at the time. Neither site, however, was ever published in full. The late Ted Sammes, in whose memory the course was established, worked tirelessly to research the finds from these important sites located in the historic core of Hendon. Unfortunately, however, the material recovered from the two sites lay 'dormant' for many years in the HADAS stores and was in danger of suffering the fate of so many archaeological investigations once the digging is over; until recently, that is.

This book is a collaborative venture by a team working together to re-assess the two major excavations carried out in its early years by HADAS. The first excavation to be studied, which forms the subject of this publication, was at Church End Farm (site code CEF61–66; National Grid Reference: TQ228894), which the society worked on during five seasons between 1961 and 1966, under the direction of the late Ian Robertson (Fig 1). The second site, at Church Terrace (CT73-74), was situated more or less opposite Church End Farm, and was excavated under the direction of Ted Sammes (Fig 2) during 1973 and 1974. In addition to the work he carried out on site, Ted also devoted considerable energy and enthusiasm to researching the finds recovered from each of these

Fig 1: Ian G Robertson, 1943–2003

excavations. The archive of Church Terrace is currently under examination by the students on the Birkbeck FCE course, and a full report is in preparation. The reports on each site are to be seen as two parts of a unified whole, with a consideration of both excavations in their wider local and regional context forming an integral part of the second publication.

This report, which was planned and written by members of the post-excavation course, begins by outlining the background of the site and the ways in which the class tackled the problems of working on an excavation archive some 30 years old. A summary of the documentary evidence and a discussion of the building history utilise both written records and surviving photographs. All the various strands of evidence are then brought together to provide a broad narrative covering the site history, from the Roman period to the time of excavation. This is followed by a series of essays on various aspects of the finds, showing how they throw light on the many people who lived and worked here over some 400 years.

Fig 2: Ted Sammes, 1920–1998

■ The first HADAS excavation

Geraldine Missig

In 1961, with the knowledge that the land was to be included in a development of public buildings, the owner of Church End Farm and Vice President of HADAS, Miss A E R Hinge, invited the newly formed society to carry out archaeological excavations on the site. Under the direction of the late Ian G. Robertson, they excavated at the farm in the summers of 1961, 1962 and 1964 to 1966.

The group's aims were primarily to look for evidence of the earliest settlement in Hendon and for any information on life in Hendon in earlier times. The primary goal was not an unreasonable one as the farm was located at the crest of a hill and in close proximity to an ancient church. It enjoyed clear views to the north and was well served by springs of fresh water. The earliest reference to Hendon is in Domesday Book, which describes there being 20 hides of land for 16 ploughs,[1] so the society had good reason to hope for some archaeological evidence of the early settlement.

The earliest visual evidence of the farmhouse appears on Crow's map of 1754, depicting the property in a rural location amidst fields. Although more development in the immediate vicinity of the farmhouse is apparent, there is not much change by Cook's map of 1796. The Ordnance Survey map of 1863, however, shows an extension to the eastern side of the property together with a bay addition on the north-eastern front and a glazed area to the south-eastern rear of the property. There are new buildings in the farmhouse complex and the larger, newly built Church End House appears to the south-west of the old farmhouse, the new home of the leasehold proprietors. An indenture dated 28th September 1874 describes the agriculture at Church End Farm as a combination of arable and pasture.

Even before the new Church End House was built, the old one seems to have been converted into two cottages. This is supported by the Ordnance Survey map of 1914, which depicts the property split, with a different configuration again showing on the later 1936 OS map. During World War II, the old farmhouse was bombed and subsequently demolished. In the intervening years until the excavation, a greenhouse stood on the furthest eastern section of what was the house. The remainder of the house area accumulated general rubbish.

The Church End Farm excavation was divided into three sites. Site 1 comprised the area of the old farmhouse and digging continued here every year except 1963 and 1965. Site 2, dug under the direction of Brian Robertson in 1964 and 1966, was an area of open land to the south-west of Site 1 and known as The Paddock. Now owned by the London Borough of Barnet, it had been used for at least 15 years before the excavation for the running of pigs. Site 3, dug in 1965, was located in one of Church End Farm's 18th-century barns facing the old farmhouse to the north.

Unscrambling the archive

For the HADAS/Birkbeck post-excavation project, knowledge of the excavation was to be obtained chiefly via its paper archive. The site records consisted of folders overflowing with plans, sections, find registers, site indexes, diaries, incidental drawings, notes, photocopies of old maps, interim papers, specialists' reports, some small finds, a display book of press clippings and several boxes of photographs. It was a bewildering array as their organisation, meaning and significance were not immediately apparent. Work on recording the animal bones, and recording and dating the pottery and clay pipes provided an *entrée* into the site's organisation and generated questions relating to the finds and their provenance on the site.

In due course, the seemingly random collection of site papers had become a multi-faceted reference tool whose parts could be used on their own or in various combinations. Once dates from

Fig 3: HADAS members at work on Site 1 in 1964 (photograph by D M H Cogman)

Fig 4: Aerial view of Church End in 1921, showing the old and new farmhouses in the bottom right corner (reproduced by courtesy of Simmons Aerofilms)

the finds were obtained, attention focused on the age of the farmhouse and whether a history of its construction and development could be worked out. A scaled ground plan of Site 1 in 1963 by Ted Sammes contributed a central framework on which the growing knowledge of the site could be hung. Two interim reports were published by HADAS in 1961 and 1962 and these proved valuable in understanding the method of excavation and recording employed, as well as outlining the results. In due course, it was possible to divide the history of the site into broad phases, based on the dating of pottery, clay pipes and other finds in conjunction with documentary evidence and a detailed study of the probable building history.

■ The Farmhouse (Site 1)

The west wall and part of the north wall of the farmhouse were still standing in 1961. The excavators' chief aim was to locate evidence of an earlier dwelling. Seven trenches, A to G, were dug along the northern front of the footprint of the house. The excavators were struck by the shallow foundations, described as two or possibly three layers of bricks, resting on about four to six inches of disturbed soil below which was natural. They did, however, find an area of more solid foundations in Trench C. Seven feet to the east of the western end of the original north wall, they uncovered wood from a door, an old brick drain and a step going into an area that was once believed to be a brewing house. At the end of the season, they concluded that, although there was no unequivocal evidence in the ground for any previous structure, finds predating the mid 18th century suggested some form of

Fig 5: Site 1 bay and cellar entrance during excavation in 1961 (photograph by D M H Cogman)

earlier occupation.

In the following summer, the line of the main south wall of the farmhouse was explored. Trench H was dug to expose the foundations in the south-western area, which were found to be more solid than on the northern front. Attention focused on a tiled floor, which was found adjoining the property on the south-east side (Fig 6). The tiles were by no means standard in size or colour, and bricks of varying shades were used in the floor. Below the floor a layer of dark earth with stone yielded fragments of bone, wood, glass and a large quantity of pottery. The excavators concluded that these artefacts did not represent occupation, but functioned as a foundation for the floor, providing important evidence for the date at which it was laid.

There was no excavation in 1963 and in the 1964 season new methods of site recording were introduced. Each change of soil layer was assigned a new layer number or its depth recorded. Two-letter 'box codes' were allocated to finds so that the same code was given to all finds found in the same

Fig 6: Site 1, eastern half of the tiled floor during excavation in 1962 (photograph by D M H Cogman)

area in the same layer of the same trench on the same day. Several inter-related site indices were kept, allowing finds to be associated with their year of excavation, trench and layer numbers. Site 2, The Paddock, was also opened and integrated into these new recording practices.

With the unstable west wall removed, Trench 1 was dug along its eastern side running north to south, and Trenches 2 and 3 were opened on the west side of the west wall area. Trench 3 is notable for two burned barrel holes, just to the west of the area that had been spoken of as an old brewing house (Fig 7). Further trenches were located to the west of the tiled floor found in 1962, the parallel stratigraphy suggesting that area was developed at the same time. Beyond the tiled floor, areas of cobbles were found, which, on the basis of finds stratified below them, were probably laid at a similar date.

After the removal of the greenhouse on the eastern end of the property, Trenches 17 to 24 were dug. These were in part located along the south line of the old greenhouse, extending eastwards a short way beyond the line of the unexcavated eastern wall, an area shown as glazed on the 1863 Ordnance Survey map and found to be traversed by drain-like features. Approximately seven feet from the eastern edge of Trench 20, a square structure about two feet wide was excavated, which could have held a copper for laundry.[2]

Fig 7: Site 1, barrel hole, Trench 3 from the west (photograph by D M H Cogman).

The Paddock (Site 2)

In 1964 excavation started on Site 2, The Paddock, a small field of irregular shape measuring very roughly 275 feet by 170 feet, and lying to the south-west of the farmhouse. According to the site diary, it was covered with different types of rough grass, and it remains a grassy area to this day. The entrance was at the north through a wide metal gate, with a long line of trees hiding the field from the garden of the new farmhouse. To the east of this gate lay Rose Cottage and its garden. The brick wall of Hendon Technical College bounded the field on the west whilst on the south and east (up to Rose Cottage) a line of chestnut and lime trees just inside an iron railing fence enclosed the area.

Excavation of The Paddock was laid out on a grid pattern of ten foot squares numbered 1 to 9 east to west and lettered A to E south to north. The excavators were primarily interested in exploring the south-west corner of the field in order to try and find evidence of a small house or other structure shown on Crow's map of 1754 and the road or made-up surface which appeared to surround it. They were also interested in the area of the line of trees running towards the Technical College and an area in the centre of the field showing patches of lighter coloured grass.

In Trench 5C there was evidence for a ditch, which the site records calls a foundation trench. The dates associated with this feature and the layers beneath it span the 17th to 19th centuries. Evidence for drains was found in Trenches 6C and 6B as well as another ditch feature. The drains appear to have been part of the same system and the excavators hoped to date the tile of the drains, and trace the run of the main drain to the field's western boundary, thereby establishing its extent at that date and relevance to any possible house the site. However, no dating of the tiles is noted in the records and no evidence of the drain's continuation was found, so the field boundary was thought to have been further east when the drains were laid. A photograph of the drains suggests that they may date to the 19th century.

The grid pattern of Site 2 established in 1964 was extended in 1966 as further excavation was undertaken. The effects of tree roots had caused considerable disturbance in the trench closest to the line of trees bounding the field. There were other indications of ground disturbance, with cross-joining sherds of pottery found in different layers and even trenches. An unmeasured spread of white clay containing a small sherd from a jug in London-type ware, dating to *c.* 1080-1350 was found in the bottom of Trench 7D, the earliest post-Roman find on any of the three sites. Further drain-like features were uncovered, with a field drain running north to south. One ditch overlaid the fill of a pit or pond including finds with consistently early, 17th-century dates. We can suppose that the proximity of the old pond shown in all the mapping had some bearing on what was found, but have not attempted an overlay of the pond/s to the grid excavation sites in The Paddock.

The excavation of The Paddock seemed to raise more questions than the excavators had time to answer. The finds dates were very mixed, which is not surprising considering the evidence for disturbance from scattered, joining pottery sherds, and the number of drains, ditches, pits and possible ponds. No conclusive evidence was found for the small house or other structure on Crow's map of 1754, which had disappeared by the time of Cook's map of 1796. It seems, in review of Crow's map, that the structure was probably on the 'waste' adjacent to the roadway and may have been a temporary shed or housing for agricultural use, and not a dwelling. Whatever the provenance, and casual dumping into ponds or adjacent marshy ground is one possibility, the lower layers of Trench 7A have mainly 16th- and 17th-century finds, whilst the lower layers of Trench 6B mostly date to the18th century.

The Barn (Site 3)

The New Model Dairy at Church End Farm was scheduled for demolition in the summer of 1965. No digging was planned on Sites 1 and 2 so that HADAS members could be available to step in and save any artefacts and/or draw any features as needed. In the event no such work was considered necessary, and they instead opened a small north-south trench with a small eastern extension in a brick and timber-framed extension to the old barn, just across the narrow yard from the northern front of the old farmhouse. The south end and east extension are described in the site index as a floor surface (floorboards) resting on layers of brick dust, rubble and make-up. Although relatively little pottery or other household goods were found, the trench was the source of one of the highest concentrations of animal bones of the three sites (rat and other small, light and generally unbutchered bones). It was also the only trench in which brick dust or brick rubble was found, which is of some interest since Church End Farm was almost certainly occupied from the mid to the late 18th century by a bricklayer.

The last Hendon farm

Fig 8: Site 3, the Barn, taken as part of the 1965 photo-survey.

■ Looking back over the excavation records

It was never a foregone conclusion that all the surviving papers could be drawn together to produce a coherent report 40 years after an excavation carried out in the 1960s. That it has been possible is a tribute to the quality of the site records and the scope they hold for cross-referencing to extract as much information as possible. Two years into the excavation, the records being taken on site increased in both quantity and sophistication, providing more extensive and accessible data with which the excavation could be recreated. However, some ambiguity resulted from the use of layers as the main unit of excavation, while the 'box code' was the main criterion for dating purposes. A layer could contain several box codes whose parameters and relationships were uncertain and whose dates could be quite different.

In any event, the more complete records provided the opportunity to use the information in a variety of ways, allowing us to analyse the type, function, occurrence, location or proportional relationships of the finds and to recreate the features of the trenches. Taking that opportunity has raised all sorts of questions that were not apparent to the excavators, such as 'why were so many bird pots found at Church End Farm?' It has also given different answers from those initially offered by the excavators. Instead of thinking of Church End Farm as a mid 18th-century structure, re-examining the records allows us to see the farm as an organic unit created at some time in the early to mid 17th century, expanding and amending its appearance and functions according to the various needs and wants of its many occupants.

The last Hendon farm
CHAPTER 2:

SETTING THE SCENE

Christopher Willey

■ The location of the sites

The excavations of 1961-66 took place on land holdings that once formed part of Church End Farm. In its latest incarnation, from the late 19th century, the farm was associated with and eventually jointly owned with the Model Dairy Farm, which was built in the late 1880s on land immediately to the north of Church End Farm's yard areas. A couple of the Model Dairy Farm buildings still survive at the top of Greyhound Hill today. Church End Farm's yard enclosures opened off Church End, immediately below the present Church House. The yard area was known up to the time of redevelopment in the 1960s as Hinge's Yard, after its last owners who appear to have taken a farm let on Church End Farm in the mid 1890s and who subsequently became freehold owners of the combined holding. The principal excavation (Site 1) was that of Church End Farm farmhouse, the precursor to Church End House, which was demolished in the 1960s. It was the main residential focus for the economic management of Church End Farm from the time it was built, which is now believed to have been in the early 17th century, to the early 1850s, a span of more than 200 years. In 1961, the site of the farmhouse, together with that of its successor, was shortly to be used for the extension of Hendon Technical College.

Miss A E R Hinge, the last owner of the farm, gave Ted Sammes three photographs of the north elevations of the farmhouse, (which also included partial views of the yard), together with a sequence

Fig 9: Photograph taken in 1937 by A C Cooper showing the west gable of the farmhouse, yard and farm buildings from the site of the proposed Technical College (reproduced by courtesy of LBBLSA)

of prints of the south 'garden' elevations. Her support for and involvement with the excavation ensured that Site 1 was dug on the exact site of the historic Church End Farm farmhouse.

Documentary sources known to the excavation team had suggested that Church End Farm might be the oldest of the three large farms extending from the village centre focused around St Mary's Church. This made it an important site for the newly formed HADAS, with the investigation of Hendon's Saxon past their chief aim, because it lay within the area of potential Saxon settlement. Documentary evidence collected and recorded by Ted Sammes supported the picture of the old farmhouse as the centre of the economic unit of Church End Farm, the land holdings of which he was able to establish with some success. Recent research seems to confirm that the buildings fronting Hinge's Yard were associated with the general running and management of Church End Farm, as a single farm or 'estate'. This is important in view of the archaeology of the two buildings excavated (Church End Farm farmhouse and the barn opposite the house).

The excavation reports produced in 1961 and 1962 are an important source of information on the excavators' 'feel' for the farmhouse, its use and occupation. Unfortunately, much of the local knowledge that must have been important in providing a context for the original excavation is not recorded in the archive. To some extent this can be remedied by post-excavation analysis and new documentary research.

The excavation of Site 2 in 1965 was intended as a trial to find evidence of an earlier structure apparently shown on 18th-century mapping. Known as The Paddock since the 1890s, this land was a remnant of the eastern part of what was known in the 18th and 19th centuries as The Hall Field. It was kept as a public open space after Hendon Technical Institute was built in 1937 and remains so today. Originally The Hall Field had bordered the immediate areas, gardens or offices of Church End Farm farmhouse and the excavation team very probably knew of The Paddock's long association with the farm. The excavation, near the boundary with The Burroughs, and a little distance from the old farmhouse, produced a wealth of finds, but did not add very much to our understanding of the wider site history.

■ The lie of the land

The natural geology in the area of the three sites consists of Dollis Hill gravel and London clay formation, which is described by the British Geological Survey as undivided, silty in part.[3] A sketch of the geology is given in the 1989 HADAS publication, 'A Place in Time'.[4] Analysis of soil samples from Sites 1 and 2 identified both green and brown clay intermixed with coarse or yellow sand and some fine gravel. It is not completely clear whether these samples represented the natural deposits. Commercial gravel extraction from fields close to St Mary's Church is known to have taken place in the early 19th century.[5] The three sites are all located on the plateau occupied by St Mary's Church Hendon, at or above the 275 feet contour line given on the 1:25 000 Second Series Ordnance Survey map. The Church End Farm field holdings run westwards, to the south and west of the previous Hall Lane, on ground falling approximately 125 feet to the boundary of the Silk Stream tributary.

■ What kind of farm?

Church End Farm seems to have originated as a single farmstead, close to the parish church and the centre of Hendon village at Church End, although the farmhouse apparently lost its status as the home of the tenant proprietor in the early 1850s. The clustering of farms with all their associated buildings, yards and gardens at Church End must have been one of the principal features of the village and its central main thoroughfare. They must have given a very rural appearance to a village that, from the 17th to early 19th centuries, was rather off the beaten track in the wider London hinterland.

The farmstead comprised farmhouse, yards, and buildings arranged in north and south 'ranges' each side of the main east-west axis of its yard enclosures. It followed a 'parallel' plan, which would have given the older part of Church End Farm the appearance of a 'street', a form associated with small farms with few buildings.[6] It lacks any kind of structure designed to shelter a yard,[7] which may not have been that unusual for a village in Middlesex. By the late 19th and early 20th centuries, the size and length of the yard and the final development of the buildings would have given the layout integrity and a clear sense of place, making up for the lack of a more conventional arrangement around a central enclosure.

A hand-coloured estate plan of 1789 shows the yard area running west off Church End for about 65 metres to what appears to have been a gate leading to another enclosure or inner yard, immediately beyond the western gable of Church End Farm farmhouse.[8] This yard and its buildings are laid out more for convenience than according to the formal planning typical of the later 18th century.[9] The estate plan, however, and the known 18th-century layout that formed the basis of the later order of the north range of buildings, give little idea of the probably more chaotic appearance of the 17th- and early 18th-century farmstead.[10]

■ The historical context

The other known post-medieval farms centred on Church End and the parish church of Hendon St Mary included Church Farm, whose farmhouse on the opposite side of Hall Lane (now Church Farmhouse Museum) is mainly 17th-century in date, and Coles Farm, with its farmhouse (demolished in 1935) opposite the Greyhound Inn public house. The origin of the land holdings traditionally associated with all these farms ultimately remains obscure,[11] but there is evidence to suggest continuity from the mid 18th century, with a strong hint that the 18th-century forms of land use and agreement had their beginnings much earlier, in the mid 17th century. In this context political affiliation and custom could have cemented the continuity of farm lets resting with particular families.

The economic concerns of the post-medieval Church End community are likely to have been inextricably linked with the demands and opportunities presented by its close proximity to London. The relationship of London to the nation as a whole and to its more immediate environs has been recently re-assessed by the late Roy Porter. He summarised the population of the capital as rising, in round figures, from 200,000 in 1600 to 400,000 in 1650 and to 575,000 by the end of the century. In 1750 the population had risen to 675,000 and to 900,000 by 1801, when the first census provides a definite figure.[12] Porter notes that London had an unquenchable appetite for country produce which stimulated dairying, market gardening, local specialization and new business chains among graziers, fruiterers and poulterers. This, by example, had a marked effect on growth in the riverside parishes around Fulham, Hammersmith and Battersea, and a reference from the turn of the 16th century identifies the capital as still fed 'principallie … from some fewe shires neare adioyninge'.[13] As well as foodstuffs, other commodities and services were provided from the immediate London hinterland, with hay production, and stud and horse training facilities (certainly by the 19th century), features of the local Middlesex rural economy.

The site of Church End Farm farmhouse, as excavated in 1961-66, and the standing barn immediately opposite were survivals of a farmstead situated close to the centre of a rural community that lived and worked in the environs of Church End. By the beginning of the 18th century, the farm was very likely to have been concerned in wider regional production for the London market. An evocative image of a Middlesex farmstead in 1715 is illustrated in Harvey, 1970,[14] believed by the author to be the first extant contemporary picture of an English farmstead. It shows timber-framed, tiled and weatherboarded buildings (farmhouse, barns and housing for livestock) around a yard. Its similar location and size at 203 acres, hints at what Church End Farm may have looked like in the later 17th and early 18th century.

The last Hendon farm
CHAPTER 3:

THE FARM AND ITS OCCUPANTS

Christopher Willey

■ Farmer, husbandman and bricklayer

A number of important documentary sources and maps provide invaluable information on the buildings, farm lets and tenancies in Church End from the 18th century onwards. These are outlined in Appendix 1. In the mid 18th century the holdings and tenants in and around Church End were recorded in the Catalogue of Sale for the Parish Lands of Hendon of 1754/56.[15] The holdings of the three principal Church End farms are shown in Fig 10, based on a combination of the tenancy, map and land use information contained in the Catalogue with Messeder's map of 1783. This is a copy of a map originally produced in 1754, which corresponds in substantive detail with the field pattern shown in Crow's map of the same year[16] These tenant farmers were the 'principals' of the working agricultural economy, concerned with the primary outputs of their holdings, but also sometimes working with or for their landlord. For example, gravel extraction or the supply of timber might be a matter of agreement

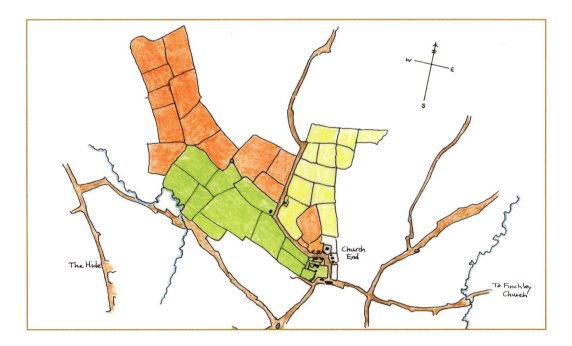

Fig 10: Reconstruction by Christopher Willey of the three main farms at Church End in the mid 18th century, based on information in the Catalogue with Messeder's copy (1783) of the 1754 Messeder map. (Holdings coloured green belong to Church End Farm, red to Church Farm and yellow to Coles Farm)

between landlord and tenant, where ownership of the resource rested with one, but the labour to access or use it was held by the other. The 'principal' farmer in an early modern village environment did not have to live on the farmstead or in the farmhouse. It seems probable, however, that most did.

The history of the occupation of the farmhouse at Church End Farm is a little obscure. The number of sources giving information on occupation improves for the 19th century, but facts remain elusive. Personal records are lacking, and census, tithe and rate accounts generally relate a name or family to a general location, rather than a house. A comprehensive history of the farmhouse's occupation and use is probably now out of our reach, unless additional documentary sources can be found. Nonetheless, we can say with some confidence that the farmhouse was likely to have been the home of the tenant farmer working Church End Farm for most of the 18th century. Its principal tenant between 1742 and 1791 is identified as Thomas Nicholl, a farmer and also a bricklayer/brickmaker, by a lease grant made in 1742.[17]

A copy of a Catalogue of Sale prepared in 1754–56[18] also contains a longhand note to the effect that Thomas Nicholl was a bricklayer (Fig 11). Further corroboration comes from an Indenture and Bargain of Sale of 11th April 1763 between a certain Andrew Reginer the Elder of Hampstead and Thomas Nicoll, here described as a 'Husbandman and Bricklayer'.[19] The indenture also records Thomas Nicholl's purchase of 26 perches of 'garden ground' close to his farmhouse and adjoining the farm's principal barn across the yard.[20] Its form of legal description suggests that this piece of land was clear of buildings at the time. Later, it is associated with a freehold cottage and premises at Church End, Hendon, in an Abstract of the Title of Mrs William Bayley. This document supported a conveyance completed in June 1876 when the property was purchased by C F Hancock of Hendon

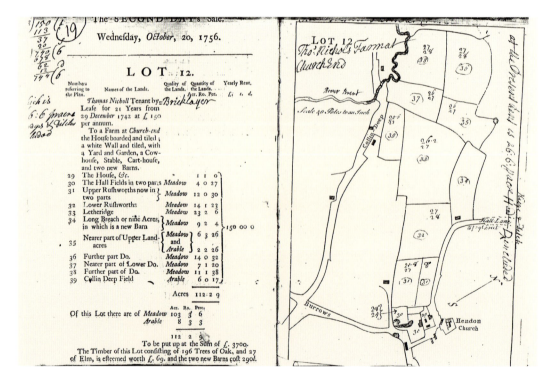

Fig 11: Catalogue of Sale of 1754–56, showing Church End Farm under the tenancy of Thomas Nicholl, 'bricklayer' (reproduced by permission of LBBLSA)

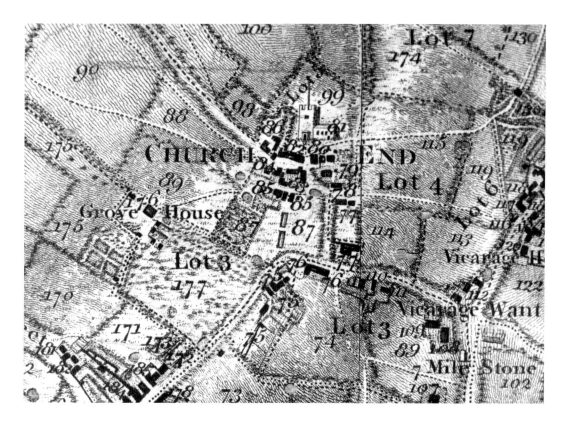

Fig 12: Detail of Cook's map of 1796, numerically referenced to the accompanying Field Book (reproduced by permission of LBBLSA)

Hall, now the owner of the land on which the Model Dairy Farm was to be built in the 1880s. With documentary sources and mapping for 1789 and 1863, the title abstract supports the identification of the parcel of land purchased by Thomas in 1763 with the site occupied by two conjoined cottages, immediately to the east of the barn. While the precise date of building is uncertain, the cottage referred to in the abstract is believed to be one of those shown in a watercolour by Thomas Bailey of c 1800.[21] Stylistically the cottages depicted appear to be of mid 18th-century date.

The farm tenancy appears to have passed away from the direct line of the Nicholls to a William Geeves Jnr in 1791,[22] probably the year of Thomas' death. Thomas Nicholl's immediate family, through his son Joseph, granddaughters Ann and Frances, and at least one great grandson (Ann's son William Bayley Jnr), remained associated with the adjacent plots of freehold land on the north side of the farm yard. At least one of the cottages remained in family ownership until 1876, bequeathed by William Jnr to his wife Charlotte. From the title documents the cottages appear to have been inherited, one apiece, by Joseph Nicholl's daughters Frances and Ann, probably at the time of his death in 1822. It seems likely that Thomas Nicholl purchased the land (and possibly built the cottages himself) as an inheritance for his family, suggesting that, by the 1760s, the household had accumulated some considerable wealth. This is borne out, to a small degree, by some of the excavated finds from this period, including a quantity of high quality ceramics.

By now, the farmhouse itself had probably been both extended and sub-divided into two family homes. With the new cottages nearby, the eastern end of the farmyard would have had something of a street-like character. A reference to 'Down the Yard, two Dwelling Houses' from a 1796 Field Book[23] may indicate an early separation of the accommodation within the farmhouse, although it could simply be a reference to the two new cottages. However, the newer cottages were positioned closer to the Church End entrance of the farmyard, and pre-1939-45 photography of the yard front of the farmhouse shows two matching entrances with panelled doors, which would fit in with an internal separation of the farmhouse (Fig 13). The whole façade looks, on stylistic grounds, to be datable to the mid 18th century, possibly the late 1750s or 1760s, and there is no reason why these two entrances should not originally have been a part of it. If they were, the mid 18th-century form of the farmhouse may have been deliberately designed to meet the needs of a new generation (Thomas Nicholl's heir, Joseph Nicholl, was born in 1748 or 1749), other family or business requirements, or was perhaps an estate improvement agreed with or initiated by the agents of the Lord of the Manor. This 'new building' certainly represented a substantial investment of both money and effort.

Fig 13: Photograph predating World War II, showing the yard front and farmhouse façade with two matching entrances

The location, character and status of the farmhouse suggest that Nicholl and his family occupied it as a working residence, or at least part of it. The association with freehold land in the immediate vicinity seems to reinforce a strong Nicholl family connection with the farmhouse and Church End at this time.

Thomas Browne, land agent for the then Lord of the Manor of Hendon, the Earl of Powys, gives us an insight into Thomas' character and circumstances in March 1753. He was gathering information on six farms whose holdings were on the Manor's desmesne lands, and giving his view on the scope for improvements and potentially higher rentals in future. The record comes in the form of a longhand notebook, and the details provided for Church End Farm and its tenant are given here, substantially as set out in the document:

'Thomas Nicholls, tenant to a farm at Church End on 21-year lease from Lady Day 1742 at £140 for first ten years and £150 for the remainder of the term and £5 per annum for Hall Meads and house, the whole sum £155. A boarded and tyled house, white wall and tiled cowhouse, stable and cart house. The barn burnt down. Three fields called Rushworth, Nine acre mead, several pieces called Letheridge Mead,

Collin Deep Close, 4 fields called Lenacre. 99 meadow 6 arable (Collin Deep Close). Hall Meads and House in 2 parts. 4 acres. 99 + 6 + 4 = 109. N.B. he has the new brick clamps at the foot of Hampstead Hill and Liberty of digging clay for which he pays nothing. This farm is near £1.10.– per acre and I think very dear lett. The land at an average is no better than Kemps which is let at about £1 per acre. The Tenant is an industrious man. Is Bricklayer. Makes Bricks on the waste and does the work upon the Estate by which means he may be enabled to pay his rent but otherwise it's a dear farm, as am of opinion on the estimation by the acre is more than [fair] measure. There is no barn on the premises. There was a good Barn of 7 bay which was burnt down a year ago and will cost at least £200 to rebuild.'[24]

The Company of Tylers and Bricklayers, a City Livery Company by a charter granted in 1567, had 'scrutiny, correction and governance' of the practice of the trades of tiling and bricklaying within the City of London, and its liberties and suburbs within a radius of 15 miles.[25] Like earlier legislation,[26] subsequent Georgian Acts of Parliament were concerned to maintain the standard of bricks used in the London area.[27] The parish of Hendon (with the greater part of Middlesex) fell within the 15 mile zone of the Company of Tylers and Bricklayers' jurisdiction. Bricklayers practising their trade in this area in the early 18th century would probably have considered seeking the status of freeman of the Tylers' and Brickmakers', in order to gain occupational and trade advantages. The Company's records show that the apprenticeship system was vigorously maintained at this time.[28]

The Freedom Register for the Company of Tylers and Bricklayers for the period 1714 – 1769 records only one individual who could be our possible 'husbandman and bricklayer', a certain Thomas Nicoll or Nicolls who was admitted as a freeman on 23rd April 1724.[29] The Company apprenticeship records of 25th July 1716 show that Thomas Nicholls, the son of Mark Nicholls, citizen and clothworker, was bound as apprentice to Henry Hester 'to be turned over to his father bricklayer by trade'.[30] Nominally apprentices had to be at least 14 and not more than 21 years old when bound, but variation from the rules seems not to have been uncommon. The term of their apprenticeship had to be at least seven years. Freemen were supposed to be at least 24, but in practice appear to have been admitted from the age of 21.[31] An apprenticeship starting in 1716, however, suggests a date of birth no later than the early years of the new century, making our Thomas Nicholl, if he was indeed this attested freeman, an octogenarian at his death in 1791.

Thomas Nicholl's trade of bricklayer and brickmaker would have given him plenty of opportunity to supplement his income from farming. The right to dig clay free would have increased his profits in making bricks for sale, as well as for use in his own building work on the estate, as noted in the 1753 record and elsewhere.[32] According to current rates for brickwork in 1749, the ordinary profit is reckoned at 12.5% for materials and 25% for labour.[33] Contemporary accounts suggest that a bricklayer, with a labourer, was able to lay between one and a half and two rods of bricks in a week, where one rod comprises 4,500 bricks.[34] Lower rates for front work would tend to be accommodated within the overall commission. Laying rates of this order may have produced an ordinary profit of perhaps £1 a week, a substantial sum in 18th-century terms. The benefit of free clay might have increased the profit to as much as 25 shillings, with a corresponding increase where more than one bricklayer was engaged.[35] Although we have no information on the extent of Thomas Nicholl's business as a brickmaker and bricklayer, and on the extent to which he employed apprentice or journeyman labour, his trade must have had a considerable impact on the general prosperity of Church End Farm during his active tenancy.[36] There is no documentary evidence to show that Joseph Nicholl followed his father's profession, either in farming or as a bricklayer, but his own son Thomas, who probably lived in the Nicholl family home in Parson Street, may well be the bricklayer recorded in Pigot and Co's directory of 1826.[37] If so, this suggests a continuity of both skills and trade within the Nicholl family.

■ Land use in the 18th and 19th centuries

Primary sources for the mid to late 18th and 19th centuries (Catalogue of Sale, indentures of lease, abstracts of title, and mapping) provide some information on the cultivation and use of land at Church End. The terminology is a little variable, but broad allocations between arable cultivation, meadow, pasture and orchard are given. According to the Catalogue of Sale,[38] in the mid 18th century the Church End Farm fields were predominantly meadow, with only 8% or so arable cultivation. This allocation between arable and meadow seems to be confirmed in a longhand annotation (undated) to the 1789 Rankin and Johnson estate plan,[39] where Collin Deep Field is again shown as an arable field, the hatching on the plan even suggesting furrow lines (Fig 14). This is the only field identified in this way, indicating probable continuity with the mid 18th-century record. In a classification from the last decade of the 19th century the term pasture has been substituted for meadow in the field use listing, with no arable remaining.[40] The western section of the Hall Fields, shown as orchard in the 1863 OS map, had by then become pasture. Documents concerning the nearby Coles Farm fields[41] suggest a more even distribution between arable and meadow, with perhaps a quarter in arable cultivation in the mid 18th century, possibly rising to half in 1873.

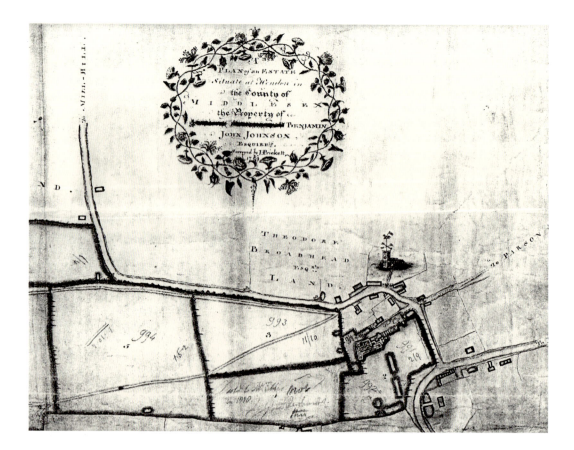

Fig 14: Detail of the estate plan of the Church End Farm holdings by J Prickett, 1789 (reproduced by permission of LBBLSA)

■ Earlier 19th-century land use and historical context

In the early 19th century, Hendon's farmland was chiefly given over to hay, pasture and associated food production. The scope for mixed farming at Church End is illustrated by a list of 'Live and Dead Stock of Church Farm and adjoining land', for one of Church End Farm's neighbours, prepared in April 1814. This records a flock of 94 Southdown ewes and lambs, 22 dry ewes, 6 cart horses and harness, 100 loads of hay, wagon, 6 hay carts and rick cloths. A similar list for November 1822 states '350 loads of prime meadow Hay. Several useful cart horses. …Fine Yorkshire, Suffolk, Alderney and Welsh cows in calf. 2 handsome polled heifers in calf. 4 capital 6 inch wheel hay carts with iron rims. Tumbril. Market cart…'.[42] The listing for 1814 probably reflects the keeping of ewes for breeding and fattening for the London markets. This mixed farming counterbalanced an increasing specialisation in hay production for the metropolis, in Hendon, as elsewhere in north Middlesex.[43] Other farms in Hendon, such as Hodford Farm and Cowhouse Farm, were largely given over to hay production by 1760 and Wyldes Farm was solely a hay farm in 1800.[44] The character of Church End Farm as principally meadow, chiefly concerned with hay production, may have set it slightly apart from its main Church End 'fellows', which were oriented more towards arable farming. It is, however, quite possible that some stock rearing and feeding also took place at Church End Farm at this time. The Catalogue of Sale from 1754/6 includes a reference to a cow-house and the 1796 Field Book gives the following description, 'Down the Yard, two Dwelling Houses, with Gardens, Yards, Barns, Granary, &c. Opposite the above Dwelling Houses, is a large Barn and Cow-house'.[45] These paint a picture of a typical family mixed farm of the late 18th and early 19th centuries.[46]

The end of the French and Napoleonic Wars saw a period of agricultural depression, and the levels of farm rents, which had been driven up since the mid 18th century, must have had some impact on Church End Farm. An adjustment was necessary and Middlesex saw a progressive reduction of farm rents as hay prices fell in the early and mid 19th century, with a drop of some 40% between 1845 and 1849.[47] Edward Nicholl the younger held the farm let for Church End Farm by an indenture dated 5th April 1824 and was bankrupt by 1827, although not necessarily as a result of his agricultural activity.[48] His successor in 1827, William Bignall, secured a reduction in rental from £380 to £300 *per annum* from W F Johnson by a memorandum of 25th March 1834, which also barred 'action for distress'.[49] The rent for the farm let was £330 in the 1840s.[50]

In the later 19th century, Britain suffered an agricultural depression, driven in part by the flood of cheap corn from North America and the innovation of canned meat imports, both of which escalated from the 1860s.[51] This is likely to have had a more restricted impact on a farm close to London, where the horse remained the chief means of local transport and distribution, and where hay production, dairying and various types of mixed farming were best suited to the metropolitan markets.

In the second quarter of the 19th century, the accommodation of the enlarged farmhouse at Church End Farm seems likely to have been split, and this may have facilitated some sort of 'artisan occupation'.[52] An inventory of the farmhouse's fixtures and fittings from 1841, at the start of Edward Wiggins' lease,[53] suggests a building in repair, with a substantial complement of register stoves and plumbing that was modern enough to be described with pride or satisfaction. From the middle of the 19th century the expectations of the principal tenants were changing, not least in terms of the status of the farmhouse as the central focus of the 'steading'. This shows the later 18th and early 19th century to have been, perhaps, the heyday of the old farmhouse. Even if the house did accommodate different households in the first half of the 19th century, it seems to have remained 'the farmhouse' to which a conventional set of room names could be applied in the 1841 inventory.

It remains difficult to ascribe specific uses to buildings within the farmstead. So little is known of their form besides building 'footprints' (apart from the principal barn) before photography and documents allow the development and re-building of the later 19th century to be at least partially recorded. We can, however, be reasonably sure that, within its main yards, the farm comprised, for some or all of the time from the earlier 18th century to the middle of the 19th, a stable, cart-house, granary, cow-house, and a large barn, possibly originally constructed for the processing of cereal crops, but latterly converted to other use. It may have also included shelter sheds, with the linked yards able to serve as fold yards. The granary probably served for the storage of grain for feeding. Notwithstanding this outline and the known extent, locally, of mixed farming, the excavated animal bone assemblage (see Chapter 5) does not suggest the slaughter or disposal of livestock in the area of the Church End Farm site. This does not, in itself, rule out the keeping of livestock in the vicinity of the yards.

■ William Sweetland, dairyman

William Frost Sweetland, dairyman of Jermyn St, St James took the Church End Farm let for a term of 21 years from 29th September 1850, in an agreement dated April 1851 at a rent of £300 *per annum*.[54] This allowed for a new house to be built at Mr Sweetland's expense. A new lease seems to show that Church End House was constructed or completed in 1853, and incorporates a memorandum of fixtures and fittings. The building and occupation of the new house immediately to the south-east of the farmhouse must have dramatically altered the status of the earlier building as the main focus of the working farm, as attention and resources were diverted away from it. A photograph

Fig 15: Photograph of the mid 1890s showing Church End House (right) and the rear of the earlier farmhouse (reproduced by permission of LBBLSA)

of the mid 1890s (Fig 15), however, suggests that it continued to receive some care, centrally placed as it was between the Victorian lawns of Church End House and the yard that was now host to a new stable and coach house.

William Frost Sweetland died, aged 78, early in 1891. An item in the District Times for 30 January 1891 recorded the following facts about his working career: 'About the year 1846 Mr Sweetland took up his residence in this district, and carried on extensive farming operations here and at Harrow. Early in the history of dairy farming for the metropolis he applied himself to that industry and was one of the first shareholders in the condensed milk industry, the manufacture of which he studied not only in England, but also in some of the great milk producing countries like Switzerland and Holland. Mr Sweetland was not only known as a farmer in the district, but was one of the most important parish officers for at least a quarter of a century'.[55]

The National Census for 1891 records that Frank, a son of William Frost Sweetland, was then living in the area of the yard. This suggests that the farmhouse and its associated buildings by now offered convenient accommodation for those directly concerned with local farming activity, and probably others as well. It is supported by earlier details of occupation at Church End Farm provided by the 1881 National Census and the Hendon Parish Rate Books sampled for a number of years in the 1880s.[56]

At some time after 1863 new glasshouses, still standing in 1961, were built immediately to the south of the western extension of the yard, as shown by map, photographic and excavation evidence. Shown on the 1896 Ordnance Survey it is not clear if these were intended for commercial or domestic growing, although it is likely that they were constructed by or for the Sweetlands before 1895.

■ The Model Dairy Farm

From the later 19th century, the purpose-designed Model Dairy Farm was an immediate neighbour, with all its buildings still standing in 1961, and backing on to the northern range of Hinge's Yard. Its management and ownership links with Church End Farm provided an immediate local need for pasture and feed. By the 1890s a rick yard is separately identified for Church End Farm to the south-east corner of the old Long Breach field (accessed from Hall Lane). Part of Lower Rushworth field seems by then to have been renamed Rickyard Field, suggesting its use at this time.[57]

The land on which the Model Dairy Farm stood had been the subject of a conveyance from William D Garnett to Charles Frederick Hancock of Hendon Hall in January 1873.[58] Leased to Andrew Dunlop in 1874 it formed part of a farm let of some 94 acres, most of which can be identified as the traditional holdings of Coles Farm. Approximately half the Coles Farm holding is described as arable cultivation, although the inclusion of a 10 acre 'portion' of the Hendon Hall Estate land described as meadow or pasture increased this to about 60%. Part of this farm let was the subject of a further conveyance to Andrew Dunlop in March 1886, associated with a deed for the building of what was to be the future Model Dairy Farm. This was to be built close to the Coles Farm farmhouse, in the area of its yards, barns and outbuildings, on land below Hall Lane at Church End, immediately to the north of Church End Farm's north range of farm buildings.[59] Ted Sammes records in his abstract from the 1873 conveyance that William Frost Sweetland, the holder of the Church End Farm let, was previously 'tenant from year to year' of the historic Coles Farm.[60] He may therefore have been Andrew Dunlop's predecessor as the tenant of Coles Farm. If so, for some years in the mid 19th century, Church End Farm and Coles Farm would have been effectively under the same day to day management. Further insight into the management of these farms comes from Thomas Downey's personal recollections recorded in the Hendon and Finchley Times for 4 February 1955, relating to the last years of the 19th and the beginning of the 20th century.[61]

In a letter to a Mr Walter written in 1955, J K Dunlop (grandson of Andrew Dunlop of Church Farm), recalling the turn of the 19th and 20th centuries, states that Church Farm was then largely concerned with raising a hay crop. The hay was mown, stacked and then sent in trusses to London to feed the horses of the London General Omnibus Company and other such concerns. He continues 'I have youthful memories of my grandfather's hay carts. Two wheeled carts with high painted wheels going up Shoot-up-Hill in Brondesbury with the assistance of a trace horse, loaded with hay, on their way to the stables of central London.'[62]

■ The Hinge family

Church End farm seems to have been leased and managed by the Hinge family at least from 1895. Frederick Hinge, who took the first lease for the family, is reported to have held Park Farm (to the east of Church End Farm and incorporating Sunny Gardens) before taking over from William Frost Sweetland at Church End Farm.[63] Frederick Hinge died in 1899 and the farm passed to his sons William and James. The newspaper account of Mrs Hinge's funeral in 1914 notes 'The coffin … was followed by several of the employees of the Model and Church End Farms' and the wreaths included one from Frank and W Sweetland. An obituary in The Times for 17 January 1934, recording William Hinge's death, aged 71, noted that he 'was widely known, liked, and trusted by frequenters of the markets and fairs throughout Middlesex, and even as far north as Leicester. Many thousands of cattle, principally dairy cows, have passed through the hands of him and his surviving brother, Mr. James Henry Hinge, for dairy companies, buyers for asylums and other institutions, and hundreds of landowners and farmers have sought their help. A large herd of cows is still kept at Church End Farm'.[64]

A 1964 photograph by D M H Cogman of the Hall Lane frontage of the farm shows the main shed (integral with the house) bearing the inscription 'Model Dairy Farm 1886'. An architectural drawing reproduced in 'Building News' for 19th July 1889 describes the Model Dairy Farm as built by Prestige and Co., of Cambridge Wharf, Pimlico. The description of the farm runs 'The block of buildings contain large cow-houses, barns, provender stores, and necessary offices: cart-house, stabling, engine and machinery houses, dairies, foreman's cottage, which together with the farm house now being built, will form a very complete and perfect set of buildings.'[65]

The 1896 and 1914 OS mapping gives some clues to the Model Dairy Farm's relationship to the buildings associated with the farmhouse at Church End Farm through their representations of 'gated' or other routes of access (Fig 16). They show that access to the west end of Hinge's Yard was still gained from Hall Lane through what had by then become a yard area to the west of farm buildings abutting the Model Dairy Farm on the west. This seems to have been on land held under the Church End Farm let. On the 1896 OS map there is some indication of passage through or near the Hinge's Yard stable block into the Model Dairy Farm's farmhouse garden. Otherwise, it is difficult to determine the physical relationship between the two farms.

The Hinges seem to have secured the freehold of the Model Dairy Farm in 1921[66] and became the freehold owners of what remained of Church End Farm sometime after 1927.[67] The farms were effectively in single management from 1895, and remained so until the final sale in the mid 1960s.

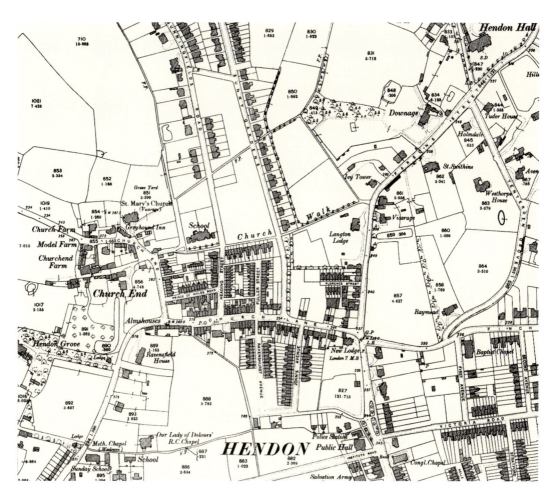

Fig 16: Church End, from the Alan Godfrey Edition (approximate scale 15 inches to 1 mile) of the 1896 Ordnance Survey 25 inches to 1 mile map (reproduced with the permission of Alan Godfrey Ltd, and of the Controller of Her Majesty's Stationery Office © Crown Copyright NC/05/40531)

Miss A E R Hinge (Frederick Hinge's granddaughter and the last owner of Church End Farm) sold successive parcels of land for road construction and other development.[68] By 1957 most of the land had been sold off, although she still retained the big field stretching down Greyhound Hill and the paddock on the corner of Church End and the Burroughs.[69]

The last 70 years at Church End Farm saw a continuation of commercial farming, with pasture for dairy cattle and possibly temporary stock holding taking priority. The call for hay would have been reduced as motor vehicles replaced the horse in the capital and surrounding region, although dairy cattle will have continued to need feedstuffs. The proximity to London (and the new suburban Middlesex markets) remained important, providing something of an 'Indian summer' for what was to be described as the 'Last London Farm' at the time of its final sale in the mid 1960s.[70] Miss Hinge continued to be active in dairying almost to the last, retaining a small herd of T T Jersey cows, which she combined with keeping pigs. This is reflected in the 1956 OS mapping and photographs from the 1960s, as well as in local memory.[71]

Church End Farm farmhouse could be seen as suffering 'social drift' (downwards) in the 19th and

20th centuries, ending its days as something of a curiosity on the margin of a land holding under increasing pressure from the railway, civil aviation and the inexorable march of urban development. There is some evidence for a brewhouse within the footprint of the farmhouse, probably of relatively recent date, perhaps even within living memory of the last owner. However, present evidence gives little idea of the scope of this activity.

The farmhouse at Church End Farm suffered bomb damage during the 1939-45 war. Although western sections of the main building appear to have been standing in 1945, the building projection to the south and east, including a conservatory, and the eastern section of the main building had either been destroyed by the bombs or subsequently cleared to make the site safe. The excavation report for 1961 recorded the post-bombing demolition of the farmhouse, but the date for this is not given. Local records, however, note that the old building at Church End Farm was twice struck by bombs in 1940 before being pulled down in 1945.[72] The 1956 edition of the 1:2500 Ordnance Survey map shows the area occupied by the farmhouse as cleared ground with a freestanding greenhouse within the building footprint. This was still standing in 1961 and was referred to as the 'east greenhouse' by the excavation team.

The last Hendon farm
CHAPTER 4:

THE FARMSTEAD AND ITS BUILDINGS

Christopher Willey

■ The farmhouse: standing remains and photographs (Site 1)

Much information on the farmhouse at Church End Farm can be gleaned from the standing remains, before its final demolition in 1964, from the site and excavation photography, and a scaled sketch plan prepared in 1963 by Ted Sammes. Together, these sources have allowed us to understand better the development and appearance of the building, or what was left of it, at the time HADAS started excavating the site in 1961. Nothing now remains of the former farmhouse and most of the other conjectural 'house' features were only exposed by excavation.

■ The farmhouse in its national and regional context

The finds suggest that the farmhouse at Church End Farm was probably built in the early modern period. When first constructed, the house was probably intended as a modest enough dwelling, although of a reasonable scale and standard. It was probably built by craftsmen working to local standards and traditions, which can, to some extent, be judged by photographs of buildings in the region and a small number of surviving examples. Information on both the technical aspects and the aesthetic of local Middlesex building in the 16th and 17th centuries is sparse and unresearched, not least in terms of chronological development. The surviving evidence for Church End Farmhouse adds only a little to the wider picture, and its interpretation is hindered by the limited regional data available. We can, however, look to rare survivals such as Oxgate Farm farmhouse, about one and a half miles south-west across the fields, to get some feel of what the building may have looked like. Factors such as the availability of building materials, and local and regional custom and practice would certainly have been important, while the proximity of London is also likely to have had an effect on building traditions. In the case of Church End, some seven and a half miles from the Thames at the Strand, we might expect a significant metropolitan influence, although its extent cannot be easily assessed from the limited information we have on the early farmhouse.

Later in the life of the farmhouse, local economic, social and personal links, as well as a strong metropolitan influence are likely to have affected building style and method. The knowledge that a tenant of Church End Farm farmhouse in the mid 18th century was also a bricklayer adds a particular nuance to the London 'effect', which can be seen in modernising or progressive influences on an otherwise relatively modest building. There are indications of good quality building work, both in the original farmhouse and in its later development. This can be put down not only to the aspirations and taste of individuals who occupied the house, but also to other factors, such as access to building skills, and the availability of surplus wealth.

■ An approximation of the building history

The illustrations that accompany the text are based on various sources relating to the physical appearance of the farmhouse and associated buildings over time. These include mapping, photographs of the building before it was bombed and of the standing remains before demolition, as well as of the excavation in progress. More general photography of buildings in Church End and the immediate locality in the late 19th and early 20th centuries, as well as of Middlesex 'types' found elsewhere, provide guidance to the probable appearance of the farmhouse and other buildings. Descriptions given in primary documentary sources also provide valuable clues. The conclusion drawn from the excavation photograph sequence is that, as excavated, the farmhouse was a building of eventually four bays with extensions or outbuildings to the south. The original bays are believed to have been those to the west, with further bays added, progressively, to the east. The three western bays were probably originally of timber frame construction on brick ground walls.

Some other considerations have been kept in mind. The wider economic development of a region and locality will have a major impact on the scope and opportunity for new building, or the extension or repair of existing structures. In some situations parts of a building are abandoned or their use altered. Expenditure on farm buildings and farmhouses, in any period, will generally be heavily dependant on the general fortunes of agriculture,[73] and the 'policy, resources and personality' of the landlord.[74] The system of farm lets established at Church End Farm by the early 18th century (and possibly much earlier) meant that the occupier of the farmhouse was almost certainly a tenant farmer, subject to the terms of the agreement between the landlord and the tenant set out in comprehensive detail in successive indentures. Investment in building, tied up as it was with the day to day running of the farm and its essential viability as a means of livelihood for the tenant and his family, rested principally with the tenant. The landlord may have had little practical or emotional interest in agricultural matters other than the level of farm rents, whether in times of rising or falling agricultural prosperity. In Georgian England, 'tenants who enjoyed little security in law but a good deal in practice sometimes erected buildings at their own cost, trusting that the landlord would not give them notice until they had recovered the value of their investment.'[75] These considerations doubtless affected the value of tenant investment and the quality of building, and would have been influenced by the individual relationship between landlord and tenant, as well as by the aspirations and resources available to the 'owner' builder. In the case of the Church End Farm 'estate', while there was clearly a proprietorial or head landlord interest in the farm,[76] the immediate development and improvement of the farm and its associated buildings can doubtless be ascribed to its tenants.

The dramatic impact of the growth of London during the period Church End Farm farmhouse was occupied is set against a backdrop of rising national population, which continued essentially unabated from the mid 18th century into the 19th and early 20th centuries. The farm's regional context is likely to have secured prosperity for its tenant occupiers for much of the 18th century. In the previous century even the troubles of the Civil War, plague and the Great Fire in London could not permanently set back an earlier pattern of metropolitan and regional growth. Resources for building and other forms of consumption are available during prosperous times or where investment is practical and likely to bring future economic rewards.

These wider economic fluctuations seem to have had their bearing on the building history of Church End Farm where early prosperity may have stalled after 1815. New building, and, at times, replacement and repair, may have had to wait for better times and more promising opportunity. It seems that multiple occupation of the farmhouse may have been a factor in the building's history from the second quarter of the 19th century onwards,[77] following a possible earlier sub-division of the house. The construction of Church End House in the early 1850s must have altered the dynamic of the old farmhouse's relationship to the farm business, placing a different value on its southern garden grounds and its immediate aspect from the south-east, as now viewed from the western balconies and terrace of the new and imposing building. Occupation of the farmhouse can be assumed to have drifted away from the principal tenancy of the farm and business and become, as late 19th-century records suggest, the residence of workers more or less directly involved in the activity of the farm.

The sequence below is based on all available evidence, from the finds, excavation and documentary records, and building history. It is intended as a guide only to a possible sequence of building, use, alteration and extension.

■ PHASE 1: 1625–1660

The original farmhouse at Church End Farm may have consisted of a simple two bay timber structure, constructed on brick footings with a central brick chimneystack serving two rooms per bay (Fig 17).

The probable plan arrangement of the two westernmost bays is suggestive of a typical small farmhouse of later Elizabethan or Jacobean date of the standardised plan form described by Braun, in which a rectangular structure is divided into two unequal portions separated by a large chimney-stack possibly serving a 'hall' and 'parlour' on the ground floor. Houses of similar character could be found in an isolated context in the country or lining a village street.[78] The pre-destruction photographs of the south elevation (Fig 18) hint at a 17th-century date for at least part of the main east-west range, since there seem to be no roof ridgepoles in both the two western bays and the next adjoining bay, which fits in with construction before 1700.[79] If the house was extended in the 17th century (see

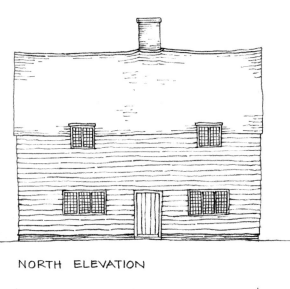

Fig 17: Reconstruction by Tim Nicholson of the farmhouse in Phase 1 (1625–60) showing the north elevation

below), original construction in the second or third quarters of the century may be suggested. We therefore propose an initial two bay timber-framed building, with framing rising from ground walls, and either exposed or weather-boarded (weatherboarding is shown in the illustration). Timber framing is more likely than a brick-built structure since a timber end frame was used for the probable later third bay, and brick construction was still something of a novelty for smaller houses in this period. The central chimneystack, however, was doubtless built in brick. This was a feature of the closely adjacent Coles Farm farmhouse, of ancient date, demolished in 1935. The weatherboarding to the south elevations of the two westerly bays shown in the photograph of the house after bomb damage appears to have been cut by hand rather than by machine (Fig 19). This is unusual to find in

Fig 18: Hand-tinted photograph of the south elevation of the farmhouse taken in 1940 by A C Cooper (reproduced by permission of LBBLSA)

Fig 19: Photograph of the farmhouse from the south, after damage by bombs during World War 2 (reproduced by permission of LBBLSA)

a photograph and provides a clue to its age.[80] A structure shown in a photograph from 1964, viewed from the north-west, is interpreted as the foundation work for a spiral staircase serving the two most westerly proposed bays, in a position which might be anticipated by an early 17th century plan form.

The brick and tile footings of the main south wall of this part of the house were very substantial, suitable for and in keeping with a timber frame constructed on a low ground wall or 'pinning'.[81] The north wall footings were less substantial, and may have been robbed out in the 18th century when the Georgian façade was built. The excavation photographs show some variation in the surviving construction within the proposed bays 'one' and 'two', but all the work is level and regular, and carefully made. The photographs also show an extensive run of the southern foundation, corresponding to the full width of the assumed 'third bay' and another section slightly further to the east, again suggesting regular and careful construction.

■ The regional context

Medieval timber-framed hall-houses in the region tended to be fully floored over, with chimneystacks inserted during the course of the 16th and 17th centuries. This provided a larger number of specialised rooms in the lower and new upper stories, equipped with heating from enclosed fireplaces served by a central stack. The narrow bay in the centre of the house accommodated the service functions of a lobby or entrance area and a central chimneystack, a staircase providing access to the upper floors.[82] It was from these models that the new standardised house type described above evolved, designed to benefit from similar advantages.

The finds suggest that occupation began at Church End Farm in the first quarter of the 17th century, but not before, which seems to indicate a new building on the site. At this date, and in a rural location, it is likely (though not certain) that our farmhouse was of timber-frame construction, its plan following the new regional fashion. As noted above, the archaeology and photography of the westernmost bays support a plan that conforms to a small building of this new type.

The post-medieval 'lobby-entrance house' of this standard plan form is well represented in the Greater London area, although the larger examples are generally asymmetrical, with a single bay to one side of the entrance stack and two bays beyond.[83] This meant that the rooms in the far bay were either unheated or required a separate chimneystack.[84] Houses of this type were established within the London region by the third quarter of the 16th century, which poses a question of whether the third bay of the farmhouse at Church End Farm, with its massive brick chimneystack, might not originally have been constructed at the same time as the western bays. The excavation photography of the surviving footings of the south wall, to the west of the proposed fourth and final bay, does not rule out the possibility that they were built at the same time, although there does appear to be a variation in form between the western and eastern sections. However, the original farm would probably have been adequately served by a two bay (or two and a half, if the central service bay is included) house, so it is proposed that the third bay was constructed later.

It was most likely timber-framed, constructed on brick ground walls with a central brick chimneystack serving two rooms per bay, conforming to a standardised plan, with the stack potentially serving a 'hall' and 'parlour' on the ground floor, but with the two principal western bays, seen in the south elevation photography, of roughly equal width. A typical three bay house in the London region would generally have one bay given to the parlour, one and a half to the kitchen-living-room, and the remaining half bay, containing the great stack, the entrance lobby and the spiral stair.[85] For the reconstruction of Church End Farm, the entrance lobby, the stack and the possible staircase feature conform to the general arrangement of the 'half bay' referred to in the literature.

Braun associated this standard plan form with a construction method of tall 'balloon' frames, which rose from footing to roof-plate. This seems to have been part of a nationwide trend brought about by a shortage of timber and a decline in craftsmanship. These in turn affected the appearance of the finished building, and may have contributed to the increased use of weatherboarding.[86] The central stack, which was previously often embellished with decorative brickwork, became 'a plain square lump containing the flues',[87] which might well describe Church End Farm farmhouse's most westerly chimney.

The two principal western bays of the main range at Church End Farm farmhouse seem to have some relation to the standard dimensions of the typical medieval domestic building, being approximately two sixteen foot poles in length.[88] These dimensions undoubtedly established a norm for the subsequent development of small house types. The farmhouse's standing west gable in 1961 was 20 feet wide, which may suggest that the house was widened, possibly at the time the first Georgian façade was built in the 18th century. The 1937 photograph by A C Cooper (Fig 9)[89] shows the third bay (here dated to the later 17th century) with a front of approximately 12 feet. This is a bay width often preferred by Tudor builders, who adopted the three yard module as more manageable and 'capable of being used in conjunction with the more up-to-date cloth yard of three feet.'[90]

■ PHASE 2: 1660-1760

There is some evidence for an extension of the farmhouse in the immediate post-Restoration period, in the form of the largest of three brick chimneystacks, sited within a third bay (Fig 20, Fig 21). This extension may well have been made in imitation of the farmhouse's somewhat grander neighbour, Church Farm farmhouse, then newly built on the north side of Hall Lane, and surviving today as Church Farm House Museum. The chimney, orientated on an east-west axis, on the building's south wall, is of very substantial construction. Its orientation and position are similar to those of the kitchen stack still *in situ* at Church Farm farmhouse, the kitchen itself occupying a third bay. This fine brick structure has a 17th-century core, with a building date of *c* 1660.[91] It is uncertain now how the proposed third bay at Church End Farm farmhouse intercommunicated with the two pre-existing westerly bays. However, a three bay house of timber framing above brick ground walls, again with weatherboarding, seems likely on available evidence. This is supported by a photograph of the house after bomb damage and the destruction of the southern extensions, which seems to show a timber end frame to the proposed eastern gable end of the three bay house.

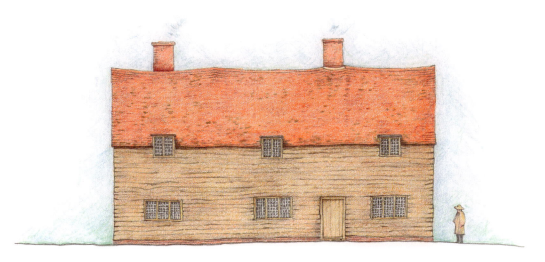

NORTH ELEVATION

Fig 20: Reconstruction by Tim Nicholson of the farmhouse in Phase 2 (c 1660–1760) showing the north elevation

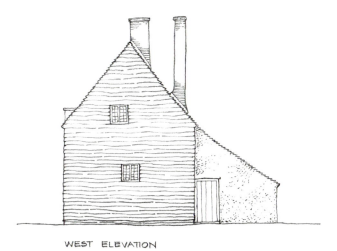

WEST ELEVATION

Fig 21: Reconstruction by Tim Nicholson of the farmhouse in Phase 2 (c 1660–1760) showing the western elevation

Messeder's mapping (1783 copy of 1754 original) shows an 'L' shape footprint for the house. The description and mapping of the house in the 1754/56 Catalogue of Sale (Fig 11) also suggest an extended 'L' shaped plan, with two linked extensions to the south-east angle. The Catalogue of Sale description of the house ('boarded and tiled; a white Wall and tiled, with a Yard and Garden, a Cow-house, Stable, Cart-house, and two new Barns') makes no specific mention of brick construction, in contrast to its reference to Church Farm farmhouse.

According to the 1962 excavation report, 'a damaged brick and red tile floor' lay within an extension to the south of the proposed third bay. Its dimensions were recorded as approximately 11 feet 9 inches north to south by 12 feet 7 inches east to west (Fig 22). The red tiles are described as being some 'four inches by two', but with considerable variation. The report suggests that the north-south wall to the west may have been reduced to allow a continuation of this floor into the extension area to the west, although it is also possible that the feature represented continuous flooring through a doorway into the western area. The report also states that the tiles were bedded on sand 'under which was a not universal layer of small shingle', which produced a wealth of pottery and small finds.

Fig 22: Western half of the tiled floor, from the north, excavated in 1962 (photograph by D M H Cogman)

The Phase 2 developments include what the excavators interpreted as an oven positioned in a corner of the 'tiled floor'. This appears to pre-date the adjacent floor area, which was probably re-consolidated and re-laid in the mid 18th century. Its position seems to correspond to a passage or throughway within the extension areas in the later phases of occupation, and it has therefore been included as a late 17th- or early 18th-century introduction, which was later dispensed with. Excavation photography shows four courses of fairly regular English bond,[92] which may support a 17th-century date for this work and for the 'third' bay of the house. A large opening to the south from the western extension is envisaged, perhaps with double doors, and possibly a 'pull-in' for farm equipment.

Fig 23: Site 1, Trench 18 from the south, showing tiles and cut-off drain (photograph by D M H Cogman)

A deeply laid drain, orientated north-south and carefully constructed out of two courses of brick on a tile base, was excavated below the extension or offices to the south of the proposed fourth bay (Fig 23). The line of the drain, if continued north, would have brought it to the yard. Continued south, it would have come to the head of the northern pond shown in the 1789 Rankin and Johnson estate plan (Fig 14), which lay some 110 feet to the south within the Hall Field. The direction of flow cannot be deduced from the excavation archive records, but the purpose may have been drainage from the level of the yard towards the south. The excavators also identified a ditch following a similar line and at a similar depth some two feet to the west, in an area of ground open until the construction of the fourth bay. Another drain, of rectangular form constructed of brick and tile, with a brick cover, was identified underlying the south extension wall. It appears to be broadly orientated north-south in line with the other ditches. All these features were probably located within the tiled floor extension area, that is, still within open ground for a two bay house if its purpose was yard drainage. All three drains appear to predate the bay constructions under which they lie, which would probably make them 17th- and early 18th-century yard drainage.

The later 17th-century house

The nearby Greyhound Inn, in Church End, gives some interesting clues to the later 17th-century development of the farmhouse. This brick house of *c* 1660 is likely to have been well known, both inside and out, by the occupants of Church End Farm. By the end of the 17th century, the 'framed walling of farmhouses was … being superseded everywhere by walls of brickwork'.[93] It is in this wider context that a date in the third quarter of the 17th century is proposed for the construction of the third bay, with timber-framing taking support from the very substantial new stack. This does not, however, rule out the use of load-bearing brick elsewhere in this part of the structure. The weatherboarding visible to the south elevation of the western bays stops in a clean line at the assumed division with the third bay; and the 1945 photograph shows regularly coursed brickwork continuing to the west of the stack up to that division

PHASE 3: 1760-1785

The pre-destruction photographs of Hinge's Yard show a sophisticated Georgian façade of four bays, the most easterly of which has been 'overlaid' by the construction of a later 'splayed' bay (Fig 24).[94] The façade fronts the assumed original three bays of the house and a new 'eastern bay' of similar width, apparently constructed on open ground immediately to the east of the farmhouse, which may be shown in an adjoining 'enclosure' visible on Messeder's 1783 copy of an original 1754 map. The presence of a possible land drain, perhaps of late 17th- or early to mid 18th-century date, running north-south through the main range, and immediately abutting the extension area to the south, suggests that this area was open ground for a considerable period in the history of the house. The roofline of the farmhouse is now obscured by a fashionable parapet, and the new arrangement must have necessitated the introduction of a substantial box gutter, with the installation of at least one new downpipe to serve the new area of roof. The window openings suggest a building of mid, rather than late, 18th-century date, with sash boxes set within rather than behind the wall. There are two elegant blind windows to balance the formal design and the photographic evidence suggests that the brickwork was of high quality, with rubbed brick window heads. The realisation of the façade, where an earlier construction had to be accommodated, indicates both skill and ambition in the designer.

The four bay 'footprint' (also including the 'splayed' bay) first appears in the mapping on the Rankin and Johnson estate plan of 1789 by Prickett (Fig 14), but given its character, the further bay extension (without later 'splayed' bay) and new façade are here dated to *c* 1760. The effect of constructing the façade was probably to widen the farmhouse. During this time the structural brick construction of the western gable may have replaced a timber framed construction that was less well suited to withstand westerly gales on an exposed hilltop site. The close dating of this brickwork is

Fig 24: Reconstruction by Tim Nicholson of the farmhouse in Phase 3 (1760–85), showing the north elevation

uncertain since there is no detailed evidence for its appearance. It seems possible, however, that the west gable was reconstructed in brick some time in the 18th century, possibly rising from a retained foundation or ground wall, surviving as a chamfered or rolled edge feature uncovered by the excavation team. It is therefore tentatively dated to Phase 3 on the basis that rendering applied in the early 19th century, possibly to address weathering, would only have been necessary after several years' exposure.

The south walls of the two western bays probably remained of timber frame construction into and beyond Phase 3. On balance, the photography shows no good evidence for brick construction above the height of a ground wall, but it is possible that demolition may have eliminated the evidence in this area. Whether or not it was built at the same time as the brick north elevation, the west gable probably replaced any surviving timber frame in that position.

The extensions remained in place to the south of the central bays two and three. The area of the 'tiled floor' suggests a re-making in the mid 18th century, with the possibility that intercommunication between the two extensions was introduced, and the north-south dividing wall between them entirely removed.

The building materials used in the farmhouse and older farm buildings seem, from the surviving fragments and limited documentary and other evidence,[95] to have been typical of the area, although possibly of higher quality than usually found in many local farms. We wish to ascribe the new brickwork to our resident husbandman-bricklayer, Thomas Nicholl. Unfortunately, too little building material has survived from the site to give a more detailed insight into the sources of brick and lime used in the construction of the new façade.

■ PHASE 4: 1785-1810

Further Georgian enhancement appears to have taken place by 1789, since a bay feature is clearly indicated on Prickett's plan (Fig 14; Fig 25). The Hinge's Yard photographs show a two storey 'splayed' bay of late 18th-century type, with window openings following the practice required in the metropolitan area under the 1774 Building Act (Fig 26). This two storey bay is taller than the *c* 1760 façade. It spoils the symmetry of the earlier work, but provided a significant increase in floor area. This work cannot definitely be associated with the acquisition of the farm by Rankin and Johnson in 1789, and an initiative by the Nicholls is just as likely. The possibility that an earlier Georgian bay stood here cannot be ruled out simply on the mapping evidence, but seems unlikely in view of the careful formality of the *c* 1760 façade. Although the excavation reports could only note clues to the possible internal arrangements of the house, Cook's 1796 Field Book may indicate the subdivision of the farmhouse into cottages (Fig 12), which is also borne out by later evidence. The extension that Messeder's mapping seems to show in Phase 3 remains in the same configuration, but with a panel of brickwork now closing the opening to the south from the western extension, as suggested by the excavation photography.

NORTH ELEVATION

Fig 25: Reconstruction by Tim Nicholson of the farmhouse in Phase 4 (c 1785–1810), showing the north elevation

Fig 26: Hinge's Yard, eastern end of the south range, including the east bays of the farmhouse (photograph taken in the 1930s)

The watercolour by Thomas Bailey of *c* 1800 can be confidently identified as Church End Farm, presenting a view of the north side of the farm yard (Fig 27).[96] Together with surviving mapping this gives some useful clues to the appearance of the farmstead in the later 18th century. Both show the early presence of the barn opposite the farmhouse, still standing in 1961, and which documentary evidence indicates had been constructed or rebuilt no later than 1756. They also show a limited number of other buildings fronting the yard, with perhaps only a single structure extending the northern yard range to the west by the beginning of the 19th century. The Bailey watercolour places a horse in front of a building in this position, where a six-stall stable and a coach house were to be constructed in the late 19th century, hinting that this was perhaps the site of the 18th-century stable. Two small dwelling houses immediately abutting the barn to the east are shown on the 1789 Rankin and Johnson estate plan and are apparently still there on the 1863 OS map. They seem to be the ones shown in the watercolour, constructed with brick chimneystacks, and with the larger of the two presenting a two-storey, sash-windowed bay to the yard front. On the south side of the yard the house may still have been on its own, perhaps with offices, enclosures and garden ground to the east, west and south. By 1796, there is some indication of new building to the east, perhaps that indicated on a north-south axis in the 1863 OS map. Eight separated ponds are shown close to the house and garden. A field barn is marked and described in the Catalogue of Sale for 1754/56, with a similar structure shown in the 1789 estate plan. A handwritten note on an estate plan prepared on the face of the then current Ordnance Survey edition, held with the Johnson Bischoff papers, suggests that this barn or a successor, then standing in the Rickyard off Hall Lane, was burnt down in 1911.[97]

Fig 27: Watercolour of Church End Farm c 1800, by Thomas Bailey, showing a view of the cottages, barn and yard from the south (reproduced by permission of LBBLSA)

PHASE 5: 1810-1860

In the first half of the 19th century, a small new extension was constructed, to the south of the new eastern bay (Fig 28), provided with a fireplace (perhaps associated with a washing copper or oven). There is also evidence from the 1936 OS map that part of the old extension to the west, abutting this new construction, was not fully roofed. This is supported by both a tantalising view of the south elevation in one of the pre-destruction photographs, and the photograph from the mid 1890s. This suggests that at least part of the old southern extension (in the area of the 'tiled floor') now comprised a possible lean-to store with an east-west axis, taking support from the 'wisteria wall' on the south side. An internal passage was probably entered from the west, providing access from the garden and yard areas to the south-west of the farmhouse. The final form of the 'wisteria wall' is adopted for this phase, including the small two-sash casement window seen in the photograph from *c.* 1894 (Fig 15). From the form of its glazing, this casement may date to the 1840s. While the 1863 and 1914 OS mapping does not show this 'indent' (un-roofed area) in the footprint of the western extensions, the pre-destruction photography suggests that the feature dated from an earlier substantial alteration to these structures, possibly at the same time as the new eastern addition.

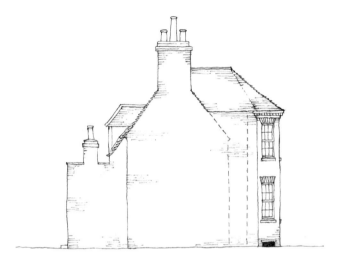

Fig 28: Reconstruction by Tim Nicholson of the farmhouse in Phase 5 (c 1810–60), showing the eastern elevation

At some point in the house's history a flagged pathway seems to have led westwards from the extensions to an area of hard standing behind the main building. It may have been associated with a possible use of the western end of the main range as a brewing house, or could simply have been a desirable extension of hard standing close to the house or its offices.

PHASE 6: 1860 – demolition

An early date for the construction of the Victorian 'conservatory' to the south of the eastern bay, seen in the pre-destruction photography (Fig 18), seems to be established by the 1863 OS map. The planting of wisteria to the southern wall of the western extensions may have been an attempt to 'landscape' or conceal this part of the farmhouse where it directly fronted the north boundary of the old garden ground, now clearly serving Church End House, constructed *c.* 1853.

The cill of a probable doorway can be seen in the western end of the north elevation in the excavation sequence. The OS mapping of 1914 suggests a possible variation of the sub-division of

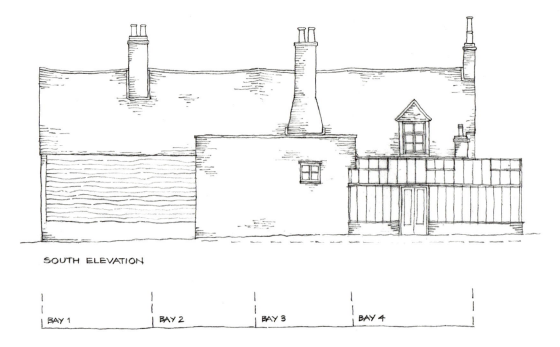

Fig 29: Reconstruction by Tim Nicholson of the farmhouse in Phase 6 (c 1860 – demolition), showing the southern elevation

occupation or use at that time, which may be associated with this doorway, probably modified from an earlier ground floor window. Interpretation remains something of a mystery, but the 1961 excavation report associated the cill with the use of this part of the building as a brewing house, and suggested that a remnant of wood found formed part of the doorway.

Undated traced plans and elevations in the Barnet archive show the probable late 19th-century farm buildings on the north side of Hinge's Yard, to the west of the barn. They suggest designs possibly based on a pattern book for farm buildings, adapted by a draughtsman for an experienced and competent builder to execute. The rather fine building immediately to the east of the farmhouse, again probably late 19th-century in date, is essentially a standardised Georgian design, following a national rather than a local trend, and deliberately 'looking back' to the Georgian architecture of the 18th-century front ('retro' in modern terms), with a finish to a very high standard.

Barrel pits were found in 1964, outside the farmhouse and within the area of the 'western greenhouse', the structure shown in pre-excavation photography and the 20th-century OS mapping as a building with a glazed roof. They may have served as water butts for horticultural use. Built against the south wall of the yard to the west of the farmhouse, the scale of this probable greenhouse suggests that is was for domestic rather than commercial use. However, a use for the barrels associated with brewing cannot be ruled out.

■ The Barn (Site 3) as a standing building

The dimensions of the barn can be roughly worked out from photographs of the scaled drawings prepared in 1965, before demolition. They indicate a building *c* 40 feet in length and 30 feet wide, including the porch projection (Fig 30). The records from 1964 and 1965 and the surviving photographs show that the barn was of gable construction, orientated east-west, with a projecting, south-facing, hipped porch. The main roof and porch were covered with plain tiles. In its final form the porch was flanked to east and west to the full length of the building facing the yard by weatherboarded and slated sheds of 'lean-to' construction.

An exploratory L-shaped trench was dug within the 'footprint' of the 'lean-to' to the west of the barn porch in 1965, in the south-west corner of the building. If the identification of the Thomas Bailey watercolour is correct, the lean-to structures to the east and west of the porch are later than the original structure, suggesting that the trench was dug in an area of the yard originally outside the barn. Material described as 'burnt ballast' was excavated beneath the floor. There is some indication from the 1965 building record of the re-use of burnt timber within the structure of the barn, possibly from an earlier structure, but not necessarily one on this site. It does bring to mind, however, Thomas Browne's report of 1753, on the loss at Church End farm of a seven bay barn, burnt down 'a year ago'.[98]

The 1965 standing building record of scaled drawings and sketches appears to indicate a building of partial or partially surviving timber framing raised on brick footings. In the north wall, these may have stood some height above the ground, possibly due to the falling away of the ground. A small area of brickwork is shown in the large format prints and 1965 scaled plan at the front of the eastern shed, and may indicate repair to the original framing in this position, or form part of the original construction design. The 1965 plan also seems to suggest that the north wall and all or part of the east wall were built in brick up to the level of the loft. This may again represent reconstruction following fire, or another repair.

Weatherboarding to structural timber framing is clearly in evidence to the western loft gable, to the yard front of the porch and to elements of both the east and west 'lean-to' yard fronts. Sketches in the archive seem to suggest weatherboarding on the north elevation, and the weatherboarding to the west gable, seen in the 1964 photography; this can also be seen in a watercolour of 1881 by John Linnell (Fig 31).[99] The weatherboarding *in situ* in 1965, fixed to either timber framing or brick walling. Whether there was any on the lower section of the east gable end below the loft is uncertain

Fig 30: View of the Barn, Site 3, taken from the 1965 photo-survey

Fig 31: Watercolour dated 1881 of Church End, Hendon by John Linnell, showing cottages, the barn and Church End Farm farmhouse in the background (reproduced by courtesy of Memories, Brent Street, Hendon)

from the available evidence.

Photography from 1964 shows the plain tiles of the main roof and hipped roof in reasonable repair, with two, probably later, ventilators on the main ridge and what may also be a later timber-framed, glazed skylight. The arrangement of these elements suggests considerable investment. One photograph shows large double doors, apparently set back on the main building line and of a kind suitable for a barn built for hand-flail threshing, with a central threshing floor inside. Large doors of this size would have enabled carts to enter for unloading. It seems unlikely that there was a second door opposite, since no door opening to the north is shown in the 1965 drawings, although this was a feature of some threshing barns.[100] Ownership of the strip of land immediately behind the barn is uncertain in the 18th century (and later), and there may have been no access to it from the barn, since it probably adjoined land in separate ownership to the north. Carts and wagons brought in for unloading would probably, therefore, have had to be backed out. The watercolour by Thomas Bailey from the turn of the 18th century almost certainly portrays the barn earlier in its history. It shows doors positioned to the face of the porch, rather than set back, as was the case in 1964. In a threshing barn, a projecting porch of the kind seen at Church End Farm would have provided protection to the threshing floor, allowing the last cart of the evening to be left under cover for unloading the next day.[101]

The Bailey watercolour (Fig 27) also shows a small opening close to the apex of the east gable. This looks like and may have served as an owl hole. These first appeared in the 18th century to let owls into the building to catch vermin.[102] The 1965 drawings and the 1965 photography, however, show larger rectangular but apparently unshuttered and unglazed openings in the apex of the east and west gables. One of the archived slides shows attractive internal framing, almost of 'twin lancet' form,[103] to the inner face of a gable opening (Fig 32). This does not correspond to the external views, which is a little puzzling. The rectangular openings may be modifications or alterations of originally smaller apertures.

Fig 32: Site 3, the Barn, twin lancet framing of the inner face of the west gable opening

The precise date of demolition of the barn is not given in the Sammes archive material, although a note by Ted Sammes, probably written in 1969 for the HADAS excavation at Mount Pleasant (on the other side of Church End), records the demolition as having taken place 'only a few years ago'.[104]

The last Hendon farm
CHAPTER 5:

THE THINGS OF EVERYDAY LIFE

■ The earliest finds: from Roman to Tudor

There is some slight evidence for Roman activity in the vicinity of Church End in the form of three sherds of pottery. One comes from a dish in Alice Holt/Farnham ware, which was found on the site of the farmhouse, and was made at kilns in Surrey between c 250 and 400. A single sherd of sand-tempered coarseware that cannot be closely dated was residual in a 17th-century context from The Paddock. An unstratified sherd from a Gaulish amphora dates to c 50–250, and is of a kind used mostly for transporting wine. These sherds can be related to more numerous Roman finds made on the nearby Church Terrace site, and add to a growing body of evidence for Roman activity in Hendon, which forms the basis of a HADAS research project currently underway.

No Anglo-Saxon or early medieval finds were identified at Church End Farm, although there is a handful of later medieval pottery. Five medieval sherds came from the site of the farmhouse, and one from The Paddock, part of a green-glazed jug in London-type ware, dating to the 13th or early 14th century. A sherd of south Hertfordshire-type greyware was found on Site 1. This sand-tempered, wheelthrown, unglazed, reduced ware was made at numerous production centres in south Hertfordshire and north Middlesex between c 1170 and the later 14th century, and is typical of everyday domestic pottery used throughout the region. The closest known production centre to Hendon is at Arkley, in Barnet.[105] All the remaining medieval sherds come from pots made in Surrey-Hampshire coarse border ware, which was the most common pottery used in the London area from c 1350 until the end of the 15th century. Three sherds come from large, wide bowls, one from a cooking pot with its rim adapted to seat a lid, and one from a large bunghole jug or cistern, used generally for brewing and storing ale. There are far too few medieval finds to suggest occupation in the immediate vicinity of the later Church End Farm, although ample evidence for Saxon and medieval activity was found on the other side of Hall Lane, close to the parish church, at Church Terrace.

■ The pottery

Don Cooper and Jacqui Pearce

All the pottery from the three Church End Farm sites was re-examined in detail by the Birkbeck/HADAS course members and recorded by fabric, form and decoration according to codes currently in use by the Museum of London Specialist Services (MoLSS). As far as possible, sherds were recorded by site, trench, layer and 'box number', allowing dates to be assigned to 'contexts' on the basis of the presence and absence of common types and the earliest date of the latest material identified. The pottery was also quantified by sherd count, minimum number of vessels, estimated vessel equivalent (EVE) and weight in grammes. A total of 4911 sherds from a minimum of 3350 pots, weighing more than 40 kilos, were recorded, although according to the excavation diaries there were originally 6096 sherds; over the intervening years more than 20% of the sherds have, therefore, been lost. By comparing the records in the diaries with the remaining sherds, it seems likely that only one or two boxes of sherds were lost, rather than a particular type of pottery. This has to be taken into account when assessing the data. The surviving sherds represent all that remains from the pottery of 250 years of occupation of Church End Farm; in a normal cycle of 25 years per generation that is approximately 10 generations of people not necessarily all from the same family.

Broad chronological trends

The pottery provides probably the best physical evidence for dating the three sites, especially when viewed alongside the clay pipes. Since it is also by far the most prolific class of artefact recovered, analysis of the data, which is a sensitive indicator of date, has allowed broad chronological phases to be established in conjunction with the documentary evidence and building history. The bulk of the pottery (almost 80%) dates from the 17th to the late 18th centuries. Although a construction date for the farmhouse in the second quarter of the 17th century has been proposed, there is a reasonable quantity of pottery that can be broadly dated to *c.* 1550–1700. At first, this suggested an earlier construction date, but closer examination of the finds shows that much of the pottery consists of long-lived types (such as Surrey-Hampshire border ware and Frechen stoneware) that could have been deposited at any time during this period. Comparatively few definite 16th-century fabrics or forms were identified and this makes a far more convincing argument for a later, 17th-century building. The earliest post-medieval pottery found on the site consists of six small sherds from drinking jugs in Raeren stoneware, imported from the Rhineland between *c* 1480 and 1550. Two sherds were found on the site of the farmhouse and two in The Paddock. During the early 16th century, Raeren stoneware drinking vessels were coming into London in large quantities and would have been widely available for use in taverns and alehouses, as well as in domestic households. There is also a relatively small quantity of early post-medieval London-area redware (43 sherds), mostly small sherds whose form could not be identified, and its slip-coated, green-glazed variant (63 sherds) made at various centres around the capital throughout the 16th century. The green-glazed slipped redware continued to be made into the 17th century and is found on the site mostly as bowls and dishes and large, wide pancheons, possibly used for settling milk. A more unusual form in this ware is part of a goblet with a thumbed rim.

From its origins in the 17th century, the farm appears to have been flourishing, its owners able to afford luxuries and purchasing non-essential, decorative items to adorn their home. While everyday red earthenwares from London and whitewares from the Surrey-Hampshire borders stocked the kitchen and the storeroom, finely painted, colourful Tin-glazed wares could be used for either serving or display, or both. By the time of the Restoration robust slip-trailed redwares and elaborately combed slipwares would have enlivened the display of crockery on the dresser and at the table, alongside fine slipwares from the Rhineland, and northern Italy. There are ceramic candlesticks, chamber pots, a wide range of cooking vessels, plates, dishes and bowls, mugs, drinking jugs, bottles, jars, jugs, and, most surprising of all, several ceramic 'bird pots'.

By comparison with the 17th- and 18th-century finds, far fewer sherds of 19th-century and later pottery were found. This is probably because of different patterns of waste disposal in the Victorian period and 20th century, with rubbish removed from the site rather than lying around in heaps and pits, and no longer being used as hardcore for building work. A large number of the earliest post-medieval sherds found seem to have survived because they were used as 'hardcore' or ballast beneath the tiled floor in the second phase of building. Although it is possible that this material was brought in from elsewhere, the range of fabrics and forms identified fits in well with the proposed first, early to mid 17th-century phase of the building, and was most likely to have been the domestic debris discarded by the original occupants.

■ *Everyday household crocks for the kitchen and storeroom*

From the 17th century onwards the ceramic fabrics and forms found at Church End Farm are those common throughout the London area. The everyday ceramic needs of people at all levels of society and in all walks of life were catered for by potters working in two major, long-standing traditions. Known generically as 'coarse earthenwares' these were not necessarily as rough and ready as their name implies, depending very much on the form in question and the uses for which it was intended. Large, heavy, thick-walled storage jars would generally require a more coarsely tempered fabric and would need a coating of glaze inside to make them impermeable. Forms used for cooking required a fabric that could stand up to repeated heating and cooling, for which white-fired earthenwares were ideally suited. Hence, throughout the 17th and 18th centuries, different pottery industries found their own market, producing the wares they were best equipped to make and for which their clay sources, technology and traditions gave them the edge over other potting centres. In the wider London area, the local red earthenware potteries made heavy-duty, purely practical, everyday wares for storage, cooking and food preparation, and for industrial purposes. The white and red earthenwares of the Surrey-Hampshire border potteries (Fig 33) produced probably the widest range of vessel forms of

Fig 33: Surrey-Hampshire border wares, c 1550–1700: top and left, flanged dishes or platters; right and bottom, porringers; centre, bowl rim

any pottery industry operating in south-east England, but were again designed primarily for everyday household use. For their more decorative and showy ceramics, people looked elsewhere.

Surrey-Hampshire border wares were made at various production centres in the area around Farnham, including Farnborough Hill, Cove, Hawley and Ash, and are first found in London *c* 1550.[106] The industry continued to supply the capital and its environs throughout the rest of the 16th and 17th centuries with an astonishingly wide range of domestic forms in an attractive off-white/buff fabric enlivened with green, clear (appearing yellow), brown or olive glaze. All these are represented at Church End Farm, where border whitewares are among the most common pottery recorded, with a total of 1043 sherds (21% of all pottery). Red border wares were also used throughout the London area, coming to dominate production in the 18th century as whiteware manufacture went into decline. The pottery from Hendon comprises considerably more whiteware than redware, which is consistent with the large proportion of 17th-century material recovered. Redwares were made in a more limited range of forms, and for as long as whitewares were being made they seem to have been the household pottery of choice right across the London area and beyond.

As a rule, red earthenwares were used principally for kitchen and storage vessels throughout London from the 16th to 18th centuries, retaining some of these functions into the 19th century, as well as being used for industrial vessels and flowerpots. The London-area post-medieval redwares, which make up almost 13% of pottery from the site, complement Surrey-Hampshire border wares as part of the overall household ceramics, but are oriented more towards the kitchen and garden, rather than the table. An unusual aspect of these redwares is the large number of sherds from ceramic bird nesting pots, the largest number recorded from any site in the country (see below).

Undecorated bowls and dishes of all shapes and sizes, with and without handles, were made in London-area redware and Surrey-Hampshire border wares for the kitchen, the dairy and for general household use, as well as for serving. Large pancheons in the 17th-century London redware would have been used for settling milk, while other kitchen forms are represented by sherds from colanders. Cooking vessels, made in both main coarseware industries, include cauldrons, tripod pipkins, with three feet and a single tubular handle, skillets, or small saucepans with feet, as well as pipkins without feet. Ceramic cooking vessels of these types would certainly have been used in the farmhouse kitchen in its early days, in the mid 17th century. In the course of the 18th century, however, pottery was used less and less for heating food, as different methods of cooking, different tastes and a wide range of cooking vessels in other materials, especially metal, were introduced. Bowls and dishes remained just as important as they had always been, but by the end of the 18th century were at least as common in refined, factory-made earthenwares from the Potteries of Stoke-on-Trent and the North of England as they were in the humble local redwares. A variety of plain bowls and dishes found at Church End Farm, and made in creamware and pearlware during the second half of the 18th and early 19th centuries, could have been used both in the kitchen and at the table. In this respect the surviving pottery from the site is thoroughly in line with the everyday crockery from households across the capital and its environs.

Jars and cisterns for the storage and/or transport of food and drink, and other household and medicinal preparations were made in London-area redware (Fig 34), brown salt-glazed stonewares from various English factories (ginger beer bottles, blacking bottles and ink bottles) and delftware (drug jars and ointment pots: Fig 35). There are 50 sherds from tall, cylindrical butterpots, made in Midlands purple ware and used in the 17th century to transport dairy produce around the country. The presence at Church End Farm of 24 sherds from at least 18 costrels or portable flasks is of some

Fig 34: London-area post-medieval redware cauldron rim with thumbed neck, c 1580–1660

Fig 35: Part of a tin-glazed earthenware (delftware) drug jar of mid 17th-century date

interest. All date to the 17th century, and most are of bottle-shaped form in Surrey-Hampshire border ware, with four sherds from mammiform types in London-area redware. Vessels of this kind were designed to be carried around, like a modern water canteen, by means of a leather thong threaded through two small lugs at the neck. They may well have been used to quench the thirst of labourers in the field.

A small number of imported wares, made principally as containers, are represented on the site. There is one sherd from a Spanish olive jar, made in the Seville area and used to transport various substances, including olive oil, honey and wine, and well known from sites in central London.[107] There is also part of a long-necked, globular flask in Martincamp-type ware, which was imported in large quantities from Normandy, although there is some debate over whether they were shipped full or empty and were then filled (for example, with wine) at source.[108] How these reached Hendon is not altogether clear, but the cosmopolitan links that came with proximity to the capital are certainly in evidence.

■ Dining in style

Various different types of plain earthenware bowls and dishes were used for serving meals during the 17th century, alongside similar vessels in pewter and wood or treen. Flanged dishes or platters in Surrey-Hampshire border ware are among the most common ceramic forms for ordinary household use and are relatively well represented at Church End Farm, mostly with clear or green glaze (114 sherds from a minimum of 79 vessels). Another common form is the porringer, a small, deep bowl with a single horizontal loop handle, used chiefly for semi-solid or spoon foods, with the border ware potteries again the main supplier (Fig 33). They are often lightly sooted underneath, showing that they had been used to warm or heat food. At the time when the farmhouse was newly established and subsequently beginning to expand, after the Restoration, flanged dishes and porringers in Surrey-Hampshire border ware would have been among the main ceramic forms used for serving meals. They provided good, attractive and serviceable pottery, widely available across a considerable area and doubtless economical to buy. There are also four sherds from plain white porringers in delftware, which was produced at various factories in London, mostly along the Southwark and Lambeth waterfronts. While 'coarse' earthenwares served for everyday needs at Church End Farm from the 16th century onwards, rather more decorative and expensive ceramics were reserved for 'special' use. None of these would be out of place in any comfortably established middle class household in central London. Tin-glazed ware or delftware is the chief decorative pottery found on the site in 17th- and early 18th-century contexts, and some pieces are of good quality, well painted, colourful and highly attractive both for serving and for display.

Ceramics for the table are the ideal and obvious choice for showing off and enjoying the more decorative products of the potter's art. In the course of the 17th century, the rapid growth of the London delftware industry brought attractive and often brightly coloured ceramics increasingly within the reach of the middle classes and those who had wealth to spare on non-essential goods or luxuries. The use of a white glaze made opaque by the addition of tin oxide, provided the perfect background for colourful, painted decoration. The designs ranged from simple, geometric patterns in blue on white to elaborate polychrome creations, including flowers, fruits, birds, animals and human figures. Part of a fine, polychrome dish from the farmhouse, decorated with painted pomegranates, is typical of mid to late 17th-century styles (Fig 36). Because delftware was essentially susceptible to changes in fashion and taste, the evolving styles can be dated quite closely, which is a great boon to the archaeologist.

An early use of delftware at Church End Farm can be seen in sherds from two dishes decorated in a style typical of the early to mid 17th century (Fig 37), found on Site 1, and dating to the time of its proposed construction and earliest occupation. Even at this stage in its history, the occupants were in a position to purchase attractive and fashionable pottery that would have cost more than the ubiquitous, everyday London redwares and Surrey-Hampshire border wares. Far more unusual was the discovery of a single sherd of Chinese blue and white export porcelain decorated in the so-called Kraak style and dating to the late Ming period. The Ming dynasty came to a dramatic end in 1644 and the export of porcelain to the West was interrupted as civil war engulfed China. Before this, porcelain had been very much a luxury commodity, a relatively expensive prerogative of the wealthier members

Fig 36: Rim of a delftware polychrome dish, with pomegranate decoration, mid 17th century

Fig 37: Part of a delftware dish decorated in the Wanli style, second quarter of the 17th century

of society. The overall quantity of late Ming porcelain found in excavated contexts from London is very small by comparison with its later popularity and rapidly increasing availability during the 18th century. That part of an early 17th-century plate should have been found on the site of a farmstead in the capital's rural hinterland is, therefore, quite a surprise. It was probably purchased on a visit to London, or was given as a gift, since it is highly unlikely to have been sold in more local markets at this date. However it reached Hendon, the plate would most certainly have been a rare and exotic item to find amongst the more humdrum and earthy ceramics that formed the household's everyday crockery.

Sherds from at least eight vessels (dishes, a bowl and a jar) are decorated in blue on white or polychrome colours in styles typical of the early 17th century, including those based on late Ming blue and white porcelain (Fig 37). They were probably purchased by the occupants of the farm as new during this period and kept for best, and/or used as room decoration. A steady flow of delftware was clearly coming into the household over the next hundred years or more, including both plain white undecorated forms for largely practical purposes (such as drug jars) and decorated tablewares. Amongst the latter are sherds from plates and bowls in the distinctive and popular late 17th-century style known as 'chinamen among grasses'.[109]

Alongside colourful delftware dishes and chargers, Church End Farm also boasted a number of decorative vessels imported from the Continent. Among the more unusual of these is part of a mid 17th-century dish in tin-glazed ware from the Netherlands, painted with a single central tulip design

The things of everyday life

in ochre, green and blue (Fig 38).[110] By this date 'tulip fever' was sweeping the Netherlands, with absurd prices paid for prized bulbs as fortunes were made and lost. Unsurprisingly, tulip designs became popular in tin-glazed ware, and were soon being copied in the London delftware factories. Dutch tin-glazed wares, however, were never common in London, even in the City, so it is unusual to find an example in the household goods of a farmstead in the rural hinterland, hinting again at close connections with the capital and a taste for good quality, non-essential ceramics. Other wares that would have been more readily available in London during the late 16th and 17th centuries include sherds from two bowls in north Italian marbled slipware from the Pisa region[111] and two dishes in Werra slipware, from the Rhineland.[112] These are among the more common imported wares found in London at this date, and would certainly have been suitable for display on the mantel, the dresser or the table, as well as for more practical use.

Fig 38: Dutch tin-glazed ware dish with polychrome tulip design, mid 17th century

Fig 39: Sherds from Staffordshire-type slipware dishes with combed or feathered decoration, late 17th to 18th century

Between *c* 1630 and 1700, the potteries of Harlow, in Essex, provided London with attractive tablewares in the form of Metropolitan slipware, decorated in trailed white slip over a fine red earthenware body under a clear glaze. Although not so up-market as delftware, they nevertheless added colour to the trappings of the domestic interior and would have been thoroughly at home in the context of a farmhouse parlour, rather more so, in fact, than Ming porcelain. Sherds from five mugs, a dish and a bowl were found on the site of the farmhouse, while Staffordshire-type slipware is relatively common on the site (202 sherds or 4% of all pottery), first coming into London in the third quarter of the 17th century (Fig 39). This distinctive buff-coloured pottery, with its red and white trailed and combed or feathered slip decoration, continued in production well into the 18th century, chiefly in the Midlands and Bristol. It is chiefly found as mould-made dishes or plates, with a characteristic 'piecrust' rim, or as cups, often decorated with a series of large round 'dots' around the rim. Both are found at Church End Farm, with plates by far the more numerous, effectively taking over the market for relatively inexpensive decorative pottery as the popularity of Metropolitan slipware began to wane.

Ceramic plates, in the form we know today, were first made in the London region in delftware in the late 17th century. Thereafter they rapidly became *the* form used for dining, and are among the more common individual vessel shapes found at Church End Farm (12.4% of all sherds). Numerous sherds from delftware plates decorated in a variety of styles typical of the late 17th and first half of the 18th century were recovered from the site of the farmhouse, mostly blue and white, with the ever popular Chinese-inspired designs quite common. Successive occupants of the farmhouse were clearly able to maintain a relatively high standard of living, with income available to purchase decorative ceramics for the table and for display.

Chinese export porcelain found on the site, both blue and white and decorated in *famille rose* enamels, dates mostly to the mid to late 18th century. By this time it was no longer the costly luxury it had once been, and was widely used for teawares and tablewares in households across the country. Plates made and decorated in China co-existed in the farmhouse alongside delftware painted in the westernised *chinoiserie* styles inspired by the Orient. The exoticism of the Far East was all the rage during the later 18th century and it was both fashionable and desirable for anyone with social aspirations to own sets of Chinese porcelain. In all, 117 sherds of Chinese blue and white porcelain, from at least 72 different vessels, mostly dinner plates, were found at Church End Farm. The majority date from the period of Thomas Nicholl's tenancy, a time of prosperity and expansion when the farmstead was in its heyday.

By the middle of the 18th century far-reaching and dramatic changes were taking place in Britain's ceramic industries, dominated by the inexorable rise of the Staffordshire Potteries and the rapid spread of mass-produced factory-made wares, effectively displacing much of the earlier, regional ceramic production. Before long, craft- and artisan-based ceramic manufacture was unable to compete. By the end of the 18th century, creamware and pearlware were among the main ceramic finewares used throughout the country at all levels of society, and the advance of transfer-printing ensured that this was the most common means of ceramic decoration by the beginning of the next century.

In the 1720s, a white-bodied, salt-glazed stoneware was developed in the Midlands and became very popular as a durable alternative to delftware. Used chiefly for dining and teawares, it is relatively well represented at Church End Farm with 186 sherds (3.8% of all pottery). Dinner plates and teabowls are the most common forms found on the site in this durable and popular ware (Fig 40).

Creamware, developed in the Staffordshire Potteries in the 1740s, had become highly fashionable and widely available by the third quarter of the century. In large part this was a result of the brilliant marketing strategies of Josiah Wedgwood, who received commissions from the very highest in the land (hence the popular name 'queensware'). As delftware increasingly receded into the background, the elegant, durable, factory-made finewares of the Midlands gained rapidly in popularity. They are well represented at Church End Farm, with 323 sherds of plain creamware recorded, accounting for almost 7% of all pottery from the site. Plates are by far the most common form identified, mostly with very simple and popular styles of moulded rim decoration, such as the 'royal' and feather-edged patterns. Much of this pottery again coincides with Thomas Nicholl's occupancy of the farmhouse, although the ware continued in production for some decades after his death. Other components of the late 18th-century dinner service, such as tureens, are rare on the site in any ware, although the top of a creamware pepper pot shows that the household was well able to set the table in proper fashion (Fig 41).

Fig 40: Part of the rim of a dinner plate in white salt-glazed stoneware, with moulded decoration, dated to c 1720–70

Fig 41: The top of a pepper caster in creamware, dated to the late 18th century

Pearlware was introduced in the last quarter of the 18th century as part of a move towards a whiter ceramic body by adding small quantities of cobalt to the lead glaze to give it a feint blueish tinge. It was extremely popular at the turn of the century, but by comparison with creamware, far less pearlware was recovered from the site, which may have implications for dating as much as for the taste of the occupants. Dinner plates are the most common form, simply decorated with a moulded rim in the popular 'shell edge' pattern, tinted blue. There are also fragments from a number of medium-sized bowls with polychrome, underglaze, painted decoration or slip decoration. Slipware was at this date considered less prestigious, and was therefore less expensive. Transfer-printing, however, became very much the standard form of ceramic decoration by the early 19th century. Its introduction revolutionised Britain's pottery industries, making easily reproduced designs available to all. The transfer-printed wares found at Church End Farm are mostly executed in blue and white and date from the early19th century onwards. The ubiquitous 'willow pattern' is well in evidence, one of the most enduring patterns used on ceramics ever since its introduction by Josiah Spode I at the end of the 18th century. Dinner plates, again, are the main form represented on the site.

■ Hot and cold beverages of every kind

Overall, vessels used for the preparation and serving of food and drink dominate the pottery recovered from Church End Farm. The proportion of jugs or bottles identified is particularly high in 17th-century contexts on account of an unusually large quantity of Frechen stoneware *Bartmänner* or 'Bellarmines', and this may well have implications for the immediate source of the excavated material and its function. These are discussed in more detail below.

Drinking jugs and mugs would mostly have been used for alcoholic beverages, while cups and teabowls, with accompanying saucers, teapots, milk jugs, slop bowls and related forms, were designed specifically for the hot drinks that rapidly became popular during the late 17th and 18th centuries.

Fine redwares, made principally in the Harlow area of Essex, were marketed in London between *c* 1580 and 1700 in various different guises, including mugs, tygs (tall, two-handled, flared mugs), cups and jugs with lustrous black glaze, and as Metropolitan slipware, often with elaborate trailed white slip decoration. At Church End Farm there are 80 sherds from mugs of various forms in the lustrous, black-glazed ware. Similar forms have been found in large numbers on suspected tavern sites in London, alongside Frechen stoneware *Bartmänner*.[113] The same combination of wares and forms at Church End Farm is extremely interesting in the light of the suggestion (see below) that the stonewares may have been used in a nearby public house. Other forms of mug, mostly with a rounded profile, were also made in Surrey-Hampshire border ware and would have been in use at the same time, and equally at home in the farmhouse or the drinking establishment. There are sherds from eight mugs with an overall brown glaze, stained with manganese, all found on Site 1, along with a green-glazed vessel and one with both green and brown glaze. These vessels, the most decorative element of the border industry, were made in large numbers at Cove, in Hampshire in the mid 17th century.[114] Humble earthenware mugs in black-glazed redware and border ware were most likely used for ale and beer, at a time when German stoneware drinking jugs were no longer imported in quantity and before stoneware production started in England.

A completely different social scene is represented by the excavated fragments of cups and saucers used for drinking tea and coffee. These beverages were introduced into Britain during the late 17th century and were, at first, relatively expensive commodities limited to the wealthier classes. Drinking tea, coffee and chocolate were very fashionable, with coffee houses springing up across London and very much part of the male scene, while tea drinking, with its own elaborate rituals, was more the preserve of the ladies. In the course of the 18th century, the craze for hot beverages swept the country and prices fell as they became ever more widely available. Clearly, new ceramic forms were needed in which to serve them, and the earliest teawares consisted of small handle-less teabowls made after Chinese porcelain prototypes. These would be used with a saucer (without a central well), as part of a set including teapot, milk jug, sugar bowl and slop bowl. It was important to have the right utensils and to perform the ritual of tea-drinking correctly, thereby observing the appropriate etiquette and demonstrating one's place in society. At Church End Farm, most of the earliest teabowls and saucers are in white salt-glazed stoneware (Fig 42) and Chinese blue and white porcelain (Fig 43), with a small number enamelled in *famille rose* colours. The stoneware fabric was better suited to hot beverages than delftware, which tended to crack and flake (four sherds from delftware teabowls were found on the site). The heyday of white salt-glazed stoneware was during the middle decades of the 18th century, until it was displaced by the advent of creamware. The quantity of teabowls found on the site of the farmhouse fits in well with the picture of growth and relative wealth gained from the documentary records and building history. Much of this material could have been used in the house during the occupancy of Thomas Nicholl, and shows that the social niceties were observed with

Fig 42: Part of a saucer in white salt-glazed stoneware with scratch blue decoration, c 1740–80

Fig 43: Sherds from a teabowl in Chinese blue and white export porcelain, dating to the mid to late 18th century

appropriate utensils of good quality. Especially attractive is part of a small rounded teapot in white salt-glazed stoneware with beautifully painted polychrome decoration in the form of a floral spray. A vessel like this would have been a most elegant ornament to the tea ceremony, and was of the highest quality.

Small handled cups were preferred for drinking coffee throughout the 18th century and beyond. An extremely fine example of a coffee cup in Bow porcelain was one of the more surprising finds from Church End Farm (Fig 44). English porcelain is rare in archaeological contexts, since it was generally treated with greater care than many other ceramics, used for special occasions or kept out of reach in display cabinets. It tends not to be broken and discarded as much as other pottery in more frequent use. It was also more expensive, especially in the middle of the 18th century when the art of making porcelain was first learned in Britain. The Hendon cup is in a white Bow porcelain made in imitation of Chinese *blanc de chine*, with applied prunus blossom decoration. This style was made at the Bow factory in the 1750s, and would have been at the height of fashion at this time. The presence on site of one broken cup suggests that the owner had a whole set, probably with at least five more. Was this another example of Thomas Nicholl's growing prosperity? It would certainly fit in with his other household ceramics, including white salt-glazed stoneware and Chinese porcelain tea services and creamware dinner service(s).

Fig 44: Part of a coffee cup in Bow white porcelain, with applied prunus decoration, dating to the 1750s

By the beginning of the 19th century, tea had become the drink of everyman and was consumed by the British in heroic quantities. Cups of various shapes, but all with handles, were by now the norm, and saucers tended to have a slight central well to hold the cup steady. Most of the Church End Farm teacups are in transfer-printed ware, with the 'willow pattern' especially popular. These are quite standard, ordinary ceramics, and make an interesting contrast with the high quality and relatively expensive tea and coffee wares used by the mid 18th-century occupants of the farmhouse. Fragments of teapots and their lids in black basalt ware represent a common and widely available choice at the turn of the 18th and 19th centuries.

■ Health, hygiene and other household needs

In the days before mains drainage and sewage, sanitary needs were served inside the house mostly by ceramic chamber pots, 179 sherds of which were found on the site, almost all of them dating to the 17th century and constituting 3.6% of all pottery recovered. There is a fairly even division between Surrey-Hampshire border ware, London-area redware, post-medieval black-glazed ware and plain white tin-glazed ware. All of these could have been in use at more or less the same period, although the tin-glazed examples are rather more up-market than the coarse earthenwares. A smaller number of sherds from chamber pots in white salt-glazed stoneware and creamware show the continued use of the form into the 18th century, although the rate of disposal, as represented in the excavated finds, has fallen dramatically.

Other household forms include part of a border ware candlestick, a small number of sherds from red earthenware flowerpots, and, most surprisingly, a large number of redware 'bird pots', a form found archaeologically across London, but never in such numbers as at Church End Farm (see below).

■ Stonewares from the Rhineland

Elizabeth Gapp

By far the most common imported pottery found on the site is Frechen stoneware (598 sherds), imported from the Rhineland, and accounting for 12% of all pottery by sherd count. The main form is the well-known 'Bellarmine' or *Bartmann* jug, with its typically grotesque bearded face on the neck and armorial medallion on the 'belly', although there are also a few sherds from plain jugs. *Bartmänner* were imported into London between *c* 1550 and 1700 in huge quantities and used for storing and serving wine, which could be decanted from casks and sealed with a cork. They would be commonplace in inns and taverns and were also found in the home. Their presence in such large numbers at Church End Farm raises interesting questions and may be related to the presence of a tavern or alehouse in the immediate vicinity. The present 'Greyhound' public house, on the opposite side of Hall Lane and next to Church Farm House, received its licence in 1675, forming part of a small but thriving community clustered around St Mary's Church. The alcoholic associations of the German stoneware are reinforced in the 17th century by the presence on the site of numerous sherds from various forms of mug in post-medieval black-glazed ware, from Harlow in Essex. These associations are continued into the 18th century, as shown by the remains of a considerable number of glass wine bottles (see below), a medium of storage for wine that replaced the *Bartmann* at the end of the 17th century.

The bulk of the Frechen stoneware (74%) was recovered from the site of the farmhouse (Site 1), with just over 10% found in The Paddock (Site 2); the remainder are unstratified. Sherds were recorded in almost half the contexts excavated, which is an extremely wide scatter. This includes sherds from at least 16 different face masks, and 25 medallions. The often grotesque bearded faces (Fig 45) are largely incomplete, but several different popular designs are represented in the medallions, including the arms of the city of Amsterdam, simple rosettes and other armorial designs. One medallion depicts a full-length portrait of a soldier armed with a sword and holding a standard or banner (Fig 46), and can be paralleled with examples in Frechen and Raeren stoneware from the 1580s and into the early 17th century.[115] The medallion consists of two joining sherds, one of which comes from a context (Site 1, Trench 10, Layer 8, HU) which is dated by pottery to *c* 1660-1700; the second sherd is unstratified. By this date, the vessel from which the medallion came would probably have been in use for some years. Rather more unusual is part of the narrow, cylindrical neck of a bottle in Cologne or Frechen stoneware dating from the mid 16th century (Fig 47). A portrait medallion on the neck depicts a helmeted male head of a kind that may also be applied to the body.[116]

Fig 45: Face mask from a Frechen stoneware Bartmann jug, late 16th to mid 17th century

Fig 46: Medallion depicting a soldier from a Bartmann jug in Frechen stoneware, late 16th to early 17th century

Fig 47: Part of the neck of a bottle in Cologne or Frechen stoneware, mid 16th century

Fig 48: Rim of a mug in Frechen stoneware with applied lion mask, late 16th century

Although *Bartmänner* are the main form found in Frechen stoneware, they are not the only one. The rim and cylindrical neck of a squat bulbous mug has a small, applied lion mask (Fig 48), and can be closely paralleled by examples dating to *c* 1580–90.[117] In the same way, Frechen is not the only source of Rhenish stoneware on the site. Six sherds from jugs and drinking jugs in Raeren stoneware, dating to *c* 1480–1550, were found on both Sites 1 and 2 and are mostly residual in later contexts. Westerwald stoneware, with its pale grey body and distinctive cobalt colouring is also found as jugs and mugs alongside 17th- and 18th-century pottery from both sites.

■ Bird pots and sparrow pie

Don Cooper

Among the more notable finds from Church End Farm are the remains of at least 12 ceramic bird-nesting pots. A total of 147 sherds were distributed over 25 contexts, all from the site of the farmhouse (Site 1). These unusual pots are often referred to as 'sparrow pots' in England, because they were used to attract nesting sparrows.

Sparrow pots are wheel-thrown, bottle-shaped vessels with a cut-out portion in the base and provision for a perch at the rim and shoulder. The Church End Farm examples are all made in London-area post-medieval redware and are essentially unglazed, with only occasional accidental splashes of glaze, acquired during firing. Although all share the same form, there are slight differences in detail (for example, in the size of the cut-out). The vessels have an average height of *c* 200 mm, with a base diameter between 110 and 120 mm. The neck diameter is 50 mm inside, with a small 'handle' called a 'nib' attached roughly halfway down the neck outside. A hole in the nib corresponds with a small hole pierced in the shoulder of the pot. These two holes are used to hold a twig or short piece of wood, which the birds can use as a perch. About three-quarters of the base is open, with a notch to allow the pot to be attached to a wall or gable end, probably by a nail or hook (Fig 49). Some of the bases from Church Farm show wear around the notch where they had been hung up (Fig 50). The base cut-out was generally crudely made using a sharp implement when the pot had dried to a 'leather-hard' state. As far as can be established, all the pots from Church End farm have the same arrangement of nib and shoulder hole as the vessel from the Museum of London's Ceramic and Glass Collection illustrated in Fig 51.

Analysis of the fabric was commissioned from Dr Michael Hughes and samples from nine different vessels were subjected to Inductively-Coupled Plasma Atomic Emission Spectrometry (ICP-AES). This is 'particularly effective as an analytical tool in obtaining rapidly, accurate and reliable analyses for the many elements in a single sample taken from a piece of pottery'.[118] The proportion of these elements present in each sample can be compared with a database of the elements in potential clay sources and the results of previous analyses of other ceramics from Britain and abroad. If a match is found, then there is a reasonable probability that the samples come from the same clay source and probably the same pottery industry. The sparrow pots from Church End Farm were analysed for 29 elements,[119] the results showing that all the samples were made from clay from the London region, north of the Thames, and were probably even made at the same pottery.

The contexts in which the Hendon sparrow pot sherds were found indicate that they were probably originally hung on the southern wall or, less likely, on the eastern gable of the farmhouse. There are few illustrations showing how bird pots were sited on houses in Britain, although Francis

The last Hendon farm

Fig 49: The base of the redware bird pot illustrated in Fig 51 (copyright Museum of London)

Fig 50: Base sherd from a redware bird pot found at Church End Farm, showing cut-out and notch for suspension

Fig 51: London-area post-medieval redware bird pot in the Museum of London's Ceramic and Glass Collection, MoL Acc. No. A24784 (copyright Museum of London)

Barlowe's engraving for an edition of Aesop's *Fables* from 1687, produced in London, illustrates a bird pot on weatherboarding near a window on the front wall of a house (Fig 52). The illustrated pot looks very like those found at Church End Farm, even down to the twig sticking out from the neck. In the same edition two other illustrations of sparrow pots show them attached to different parts of the house; one on an upright post and one onto the plaster. There is also an illustration by William Hogarth in Samuel Butler's *Hudibras*, of 1775, again produced in London, which shows a similar pot attached just below the eaves of a house (Fig 53).[120] Although we may never know precisely where the Sparrow pots from Church End Farm were attached, it seems likely that they were positioned high on the southern wall, near the eaves, and close to a window for access.

The dating of the sparrow pot sherds from Church End Farm depends on the dating of the contexts in which they were found. These, with one exception, which may well be intrusive or a misinterpretation of the context number, can all be dated to the last quarter of the 17th or first quarter of the 18th century. This is well within the date range for such pots in the Greater London area. The earliest reference to a sparrow pot in London comes from the Bridge House Accounts for 1516-1528[121] In March 1527 payment is noted 'for v sparrow pottys for the garden iijd' and again 'to William Snethe….for sparrowe pottes iijd'.[122] Unfortunately, the type is not specified, although the reference to 'pottys' suggests that they were ceramic. One of the latest references dates to 1833: 'In the vicinity of London more particularly, pots of unglazed delf ware of a sub-oval shape, with a narrow hole for an entrance, are fixed upon the wall of houses, several feet below the eave, and the sparrows finding a domicile so suited to their habits, very soon take possession of every pot thus provided for them'.[123]

It is impossible now to know what Rennie meant by 'delf ware', but only red earthenware bird pot sherds have been found in London excavations. The only reference to sparrow pots being made in London is by Loudon (1842). Describing the use of sparrow pots as 'a neat cottage ornament', he reports that 'we have seen a sparrow pot made by Adams of Gray's Inn Lane'.[124] A painting at the Grim's Dyke Hotel in Harrow, North London, dated 1856 and signed E O W (E O White?), shows a number of sparrow pots attached to a farmhouse. It is remarkable that for a form of pot known to have been made for 350 years only around 60 examples are recorded from the Greater London area, including the 12 from Church End Farm.

The purpose for which bird pots were made has attracted several suggestions over the years. Buying

Fig 52: Francis Barlowe's engraving for an edition of Aesop's Fables, from 1687, showing a bird pot attached near an upstairs window

Fig 53: Illustration by William Hogarth, from Samuel Butler's Hudibras, showing a bird pot below the eaves of a house (reproduced by kind permission of the Hogarth House Museum, Chiswick)

and setting up a bird pot required both cost and effort, so why did people do it? The most frequently made suggestion is that it was to collect the chicks and/or eggs, which seems plausible given the cut-out access for a human hand in the base. A pot with no such human access would be much more secure for the bird, and less likely to let in water, draughts or predators such as rats. So why would people want to take the chicks and/or eggs? There have been many suggestions, including hand-rearing them as cage birds, and feeding sparrow hawks in training. One of the more popular theories is that they were taken to collect the bounty on certain kinds of birds. In 1533, an Act of Parliament was passed 'ordering parishes to wage war on agriculturally pernicious jackdaws, crows and rooks'.[125] This list was extended in 1566 *inter alia* to include sparrows. The Act allowed for 'bounties' to be paid by churchwardens for dead birds and eggs, and was not repealed until 1860. There are many examples from around the country of churchwardens paying the bounty for dead sparrow chicks.[126]

By far the most common theory is that the chicks were taken to be eaten by people, mostly as a dietary supplement for those who could not afford meat. There are many literary references to chicks being used as food:

'They could also provide a source of food for when all other meats were prohibitively expensive the sparrow was both legal to trap and easy to catch.'[127]

'Sparrow bottles were for sparrows to build their nest in; that, when the eggs were hatched, the inhabitants of the house took the nest for the sake of the young birds, which were considered a great delicacy at table.'[128]

'In fact, from the early seventeenth century, farm labourers were encouraged to hang unglazed earthenware pots under their eaves to attract nesting sparrows. This, it was argued, would provide a meat diet because the fledglings could easily be shifted from eaves to oven. Truly the sparrow's home had become its casserole.'[129]

'Sometimes I would put sparrows in the pie with diffcrent things to flavour it.'[130]

'Sparrow pie was a regular country dish until the First World War.'[131]

Evidence for bird pots from excavations in London is sparse. Sherds were found at the London Charterhouse excavation,[132] in a robber cut thought to post-date 1715, and are probably residual. The presence of sparrow bones in the 'post-consumption waste' is significant, indicating 'that these species may have been a special part of the meal'.[133] This is supported by the discovery of sparrow bones in excavations at Deptford: 'House sparrow bones from the fireplace may also be food refuse as sparrows were stewed in ale and seasoned with herbs in Elizabethan times, while later, in the 18th century, they were rolled in a paste, boiled and served as dumplings'.[134]

It is probably impossible to be certain for what purpose the Church End Farm sparrow pots were used. The collection of bounty on the birds seems unlikely, since the church is situated a few hundred metres from the farm, and there are no records of bounty being paid for sparrows in either the churchwardens' or the overseers' accounts, although it was paid for foxes, rooks, and even hedgehogs. The most likely explanation, therefore, is that the pots were used to provide sparrow chicks for the table. Twelve out of the 60 or so known bird pots from London come from Church End Farm. Why should this be? The remains of bird pots are difficult to identify in excavated pottery, unless the telltale features such as the cut-out base, the nib and the hole in the shoulder are present, and body sherds can easily be confused with redware jars and jugs. The form was not widely known until Roy Stephenson's article in 1991 brought them to light. It is therefore likely that the tally should be much higher, although since most of the London sites come from urban areas, the large number of bird pots found on a farmstead in the rural hinterland may not be so surprising.

■ A good pipe of tobacco

Stephen Brunning and Jacqui Pearce

Clay pipes are a gift to the archaeologist. Smoking was immensely popular in England from the end of the 16th century onwards, and clay pipes were the chief means of taking tobacco right across society. Readily obtainable throughout the country, they were also easily broken, so had a short lifetime, maybe of a few smokes, or even only one. Since styles and shapes of pipe bowl changed roughly every 20 to 40 years, they are also easy to date when enough of the bowl has survived, hence their value to the archaeologist. The importance of clay pipes, however, goes far beyond dating. People at all levels of society smoked and once tobacco had become more widely available and affordable, around the middle of the 17th century, numerous pipemakers could be found in all the major cities and towns. Smoking became inextricably linked with drinking and pipes were available in taverns, inns and alehouses, as well as in coffee houses; and when the pipe had been smoked or broken, it was simply thrown away in the nearest most convenient place. Their very disposability makes them an invaluable source of information on many different aspects of everyday life.

A total of 1232 clay pipe fragments were found during the excavations at Church End Farm. The 82 pipe bowls that were complete enough to identify were recorded using the dated typology for London pipes established by Atkinson and Oswald in 1969. As part of the original post-excavation process carried out by Ted Sammes and other members of HADAS, the Church End Farm pipes were shown to foremost pipe specialist, Adrian Oswald, and his comments and dating recorded for all bowls. The numerous stem fragments, mouthpieces and small bowl fragments recovered are impossible to link with bowl types. By far the largest number of fragments (740) were found on the site of the farmhouse (Site 1), including 101 bowls, not all of which are datable. Far fewer pipes came from The Paddock (Site 2: 297 fragments), including 39 bowls. Unsurprisingly, only two undatable bowl fragments and 28 pieces of stem were found in the Barn (Site 3).

■ *Early pipes – the 17th century*

The idea of the clay tobacco pipe in Europe was probably derived from native American usage around the middle of the 16th century, shortly before tobacco was introduced to England in 1558.[135] Throughout its history, the basic form of the pipe remained the same, although there were variations in bowl size and shape, stem diameter and length. The earliest English pipes were handmade, and by *c* 1580 were characterised by a flat heel, a roughly barrel-shaped, thick-walled bowl and a straight stem, about 100–150 mm in length. It was soon discovered that pipes could be made far more efficiently and effectively using a two-piece mould, and handmade pipes were very short-lived. Early pipe bowls were very small, rather like an acorn cup, because tobacco was initially very expensive and very strong. An early reference speaks of 'drink[ing] the smoak of tobacco', which gives some idea of the way in which the smoker drew in the smoke in a short, sharp draught.[136] The costliness of tobacco limited its availability and circulation at first to the upper end of society, although once the newly established English colony of Jamestown, in Virginia, (founded in 1607) began to harvest tobacco crops and send them back regularly to London, the 'divine weed' became much more affordable and the craze for smoking grew apace.

Seven pipes from Church End Farm can be dated to *c* 1610–40 (Fig 54). All are well finished, with milling around the top of the bowl and one has a maker's mark in the form of a star under the heel. Unfortunately, symbols such as this are very difficult to tie in with known makers, and common marks might be shared by more than one workshop. Four of the pipes come from Site 1, and therefore fit in very well with the suggested date for the construction of the farmhouse in the second quarter of the 17th century, and are contemporaneous with the early delftware found on the site. The remaining three early pipes are unstratified.

After *c* 1640, the pipe bowl became larger, and the stem length increased to about 250–350 mm. This basic shape remained more or less unchanged for the next 60 years, except for the addition of a short, rounded spur on some types, instead of the flat heel. Most 17th-century pipes were plain, although a band of milling around the top of the bowl was common, and some pipes were also burnished to give them a shiny surface. Pipemakers also sometimes marked their products by stamping their initials or a symbol distinctive to their workshop underneath the heel or on the bowl. Eight pipe bowls found on the site date to the mid 17th century; five of them came from the farmhouse (Fig 55). One pipe bowl of this date was also found in The Paddock.

The period of consolidation and possible expansion at Church End Farm in the late 17th to early

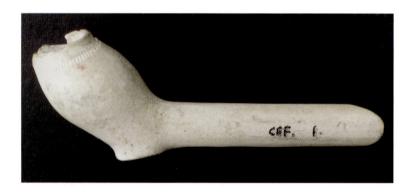

Fig 54: Clay pipe bowl from the site of the farmhouse, dated to c 1610–40

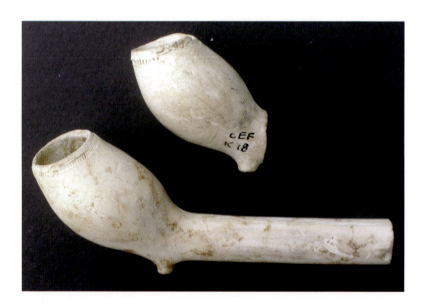

Fig 55: Two clay pipe bowls from the site of the farmhouse, dated to c 1640–60

18th century is marked by one of the highest concentrations of clay pipes found on the site, with 29 bowls accounting for 35.4% of all datable pipes recovered. Sixteen were found on Site 1, and one, dated *c* 1680–1720 came from The Paddock. None are decorated, although milling around the top of the bowl was still common. One bowl is marked, and was probably made by George Wharton, recorded in Shoreditch in 1723.[137] If this identification is correct, it suggests a possible connection with an area of London situated on one of the main routes from Hendon into the City. Clay pipes, by their very nature, tended not to travel very far from their place of manufacture. Perhaps the pipe was acquired on his journey by one of the farm labourers carting hay into London, offering a tantalising glimpse of the farmstead's possible links with the capital.

■ A longer smoke – pipes in the 18th century

By the end of the 17th century, pipe bowl diameter and stem bore had increased noticeably. After 1700, as methods of manufacture improved, including firing and mould-making, bowls became thinner, and stems more slender. The introduction of the gin-press around 1700, allowed the pipe bowl to be trimmed level rather than inclined forward.[138] In the middle of the 18th century, the *alderman* or *straw* pipe became fashionable, and could measure up to 600 mm in length, remaining in production for the next 100 years. Pipe-smoking was ubiquitous, and an almost inseparable accompaniment to drinking, as prints and paintings of the time show. The longer pipes would have been used in such leisurely activities, as they were far too fragile to smoke at their full length while working.

A large proportion of the identifiable pipe bowls found at Church End Farm date to the 18th century (34 bowls or 41.5%). Most of these date to the first half of the century, with only 11 examples definitely made after 1760. Their distribution is interesting, with seven examples coming from The Paddock, all dating after *c* 1730, with some types as late as *c* 1780–1820. These include two pipe bowls with the maker's initials 'CD' moulded in relief on the sides of the heel, identified by Oswald as the work of a pipemaker called Charles Dickens, who was recorded in Spitalfields in 1817–28,[139] thereby giving another clue to some of the London connections of those who lived and worked on the farmstead. By the 18th century, Brick Lane in Spitalfields had become a major market for livestock. In this context, an association with those farms in London's rural hinterland that supplied the capital with hay and animal fodder is not surprising.

Five clay pipe bowls found on the site of the farmhouse date to *c* 1700–40. Among these is a pipe with the maker's initials 'IN' moulded on the sides of the heel. This was identified by Oswald as the work of John Newton, recorded in Bristol in 1747. This is one of two pipes identified on the site that were made outside London. The other is represented by a stem fragment with the incomplete word 'BROSEL..' stamped along its length. This stands for Broseley, a major centre for clay pipe manufacture in Shropshire since the 17th century. Stamping along the line of the stem was not introduced until the 1760s, usually including the word 'Broseley'.[140] An incuse stamp, such as the one found at Hendon, was first used *c* 1840, by Noah Roden II and was later taken up by other Broseley pipemakers, the style continuing into the 20th century.[141] There seems little doubt that before the 19th century Broseley pipes were marketed locally, with the work of some makers so localised that they are found in only one part of the town.[142] From the 19th century onwards they are found over a wider area, and a relatively small number have been recorded in London. They were not a regular trade item with the capital, in much the same way as 18th-century Bristol pipes of the kind found at Church End

Farm. When they occur outside their usual area of distribution, pipes from other regions were probably brought in by people travelling to or from that area and simply thrown away when finished or broken. Whether this means that there were any formal contacts between the Hendon farmstead and Broseley or Bristol is probably impossible to determine at this remove in time.

■ Victorian fancies

After 1850, pipes were being made up to 900 mm in length (36 inches): the 'yard of clay', commonly known as a *churchwarden*. During the second half of the 19th century, the manufacture of decorated pipes increased, as their potential for advertising was recognised.[143] All manner of designs were produced and sold as cheap novelties or *fancies*. A decorated pipe from this period found in the Church End Farm excavations has two moulded, crossed keys on each side of the bowl, with a leaf design running along the stem (Fig 56). From the shape of the bowl, the pipe dates to *c* 1850–1910 and was probably made for a public house called 'The Cross Keys', the location of which is now unknown. Two other 'fancies' were recovered from the site of the farmhouse. One is in the form of a pony's hoof and the other is represented by part of the stem of a 'thorn pipe', made to look like a briar twig, with moulded thorns. Both date to the second half of the 19th century. Despite the availability of elaborately decorated pipes, the 'ordinary man' preferred a short pipe that was very cheap to make, and was often supplied with a tankard of ale by the publican. It was not unusual for the stem to be broken off at various lengths to suit the user.[144] Very few other pipe fragments from the site can definitely be dated to the 19th century. Part of a large pipe bowl of the so-called 'Irish type', also found on Site 1, has a moulded shamrock on each side of the heel, and dates to *c* 1840–1910. This form was made by various London pipemakers and does not indicate an Irish connection.

Very few other decorated pipes were found on the site, mostly very common types represented by small fragments only, with moulded leaf seams or vertical fluting round the bowl. Pipes of this kind were especially popular in the late 18th and early 19th century. There is, however, one fragment from the front of a bowl dated to *c* 1780–1850, which has the remains of moulded Masonic emblems on either side of a moulded leaf seam (Fig 57). Masonic pipes appear to have been introduced in the mid

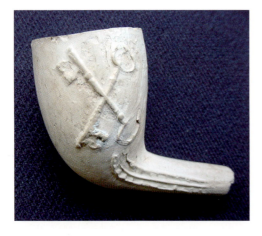

Fig 56: Clay pipe dated to c 1850–1910, decorated with moulded crossed keys

Fig 57: Part of a clay pipe decorated with Masonic emblems dated to c 1750–1850

18th century and continued to be made into the 19th, including various combinations of the different emblems.[145] All that remains on the Hendon pipe is the crescent moon and one of the three towers. Whether or not the discovery of this pipe means that one of the occupants of Church End Farm was a Freemason is uncertain, but certainly not impossible, given the Nicholl family's connections with the brick-making trade.

One marked pipe, of a kind made between *c* 1840 and 1880, has the incuse word 'Highgate' set within a shield stamped on the back of the bowl (Fig 58, Fig 59). Although the maker's name at the top of the shield has almost worn away, '..ON' is just about visible at the end, probably Harrison of Highgate. The mark compares closely with a pipe found during the HADAS excavations at 1246 High Road, Whetstone in 1989. Highgate pipes were also found in Hendon during the excavations at Church Terrace, on the other side of Hall Lane, marked with the name 'Andrews'. Highgate was clearly a good, relatively local source of clay pipes, probably among the closest to Hendon in north London.

The significance of the dramatic drop in datable pipes in the 19th century is hard to discern, although it does form part of an overall picture at Church End Farm, whereby the finds in general decline in quantity in the Victorian period and later. Certainly, there is far less pottery of 19th-century date, and the answer may well lie in different patterns of waste disposal at this time. By 1914, the manufacture of clay pipes was virtually at an end. Only a handful of well-established makers existed to supply a 'hard core' of clay tobacco pipe smokers, as cigarettes and briar pipes took over.

Fig 59: Detail of the maker's mark on the clay pipe illustrated in Fig 58

Fig 58: Clay pipe bowl stamped with the name '[Harris]on' and 'Highgate', dated to c 1840–80

■ Wine bottles, phials and window glass

Don Cooper

The excavation diaries from Church End Farm record that 5305 fragments of glass were found between 1964 and 1966 excavations, with an unknown amount from the earlier excavations. Of all these fragments only 142 remain (Fig 60). There is circumstantial evidence that a large number were thrown away, as the remaining fragments consist mainly of the necks and bases of late 18th- to early 19th-century wine bottles. A more balanced collection, including body sherds, would usually be expected unless there had been sampling at some stage. The bulk of the wine bottles are types that can be dated to the 18th century, before the advent of the truly cylindrical bottle, suitable for binning on its side. This meant that wine was generally decanted into the bottle from a cask, rather than laid down. The Greyhound Inn, directly across the road, is one possible source, and it is quite possible that

Fig 60: Selection of glass wine bottle necks from Church End Farm, dating to the late 18th and early 19th centuries

the occupants of the farm obtained their wine from here. However, the keeping of a 'cellar' is certainly in line with the general picture of increased prosperity in the later 18th century. Among the wine bottle necks is one with its cork still in place. None of the recorded wine bottle fragments dates later than the first quarter of the 19th century. Later bottles might not have been collected, although there are also markedly lower proportions of pottery and clay pipes from the 19th century, so it may well be that rubbish was disposed of in a different way at this period, or in different places.

Three complete pharmaceutical phials and the tops of two others were found on Site 1, all dating from the late 18th century (Fig 61, Fig 62).[146] Phials of this kind are common enough on sites across the London area and would have been a standard container for many different kinds of medicinal preparation. The base of a Pyrmont mineral water bottle was also found in the archive. In the 18th century, mineral waters from the spa at Pyrmont (Piermont), the capital of Waldeck, Germany, were popular in England.[147] Earlier in the 18th century, mineral water from Bath, Bristol and Holt was popular, but the imported Pyrmont water captured the market, at the expense of home-produced mineral waters.[148] By 1827 the London Directory was listing only three mineral water warehouses, as against 10 such premises for the holding and distribution of soda waters, including the warehouse of J.

Fig 61: Green glass pharmaceutical phial, dating to the late 18th century

Fig 62: Green glass pharmaceutical phial, dating to the late 18th century

Schweppes and Co.[149] An almost complete tonic or soda water bottle is recorded as unstratified. It is marked on one side 'This is the property of H D Rawlings, Nassau St, London W', and on the other 'Codd's Patent, 4 Makers Codd and Rylands Barnsley', with 'H D R' underneath the base. Hiram Codd took out his patent for the marble-in-neck bottle in 1872, although the Hendon bottle dates from between 1885 and 1890. Before Codd's patent, carbonated mineral water was sold in what are now known as torpedo bottles, because of their shape. They had to be stored on their side to prevent the cork drying out and being blown from the bottle. Codd's patent solved the problem and continued to be used, albeit with some improvements, until comparatively recently. The term 'Coddswallop', meaning rubbish, is said to have been coined by beer drinkers to describe mineral water from Codd's bottles! H D Rawlings was a maker of tonic and soda water, combining with R White, the lemonade makers, in 1891.

A very small amount of window glass remains; the excavation diaries hint that there was originally a large quantity. One piece has the dimensions of the pane (22$^{1}/_{2}$" x 16") scrawled on it in pencil. Another is a rectangular piece 3 x 2 inches with white frosted decoration. It is only to be expected that the greenhouses known to have been on the site would have produced considerable amounts of glass, and hardly surprising that this was not retained.

■ Bricks and tiles: the fabric of the building

Elizabeth Gapp and Christopher Willey

Although a large quantity of building material was present in the upper 'demolition' level of Site 1, very little appears to have been retained; the archive now holds only two boxes of ceramic building material. According to the excavation diaries, more than 145 tile fragments were recovered from the site, most of which have now disappeared. Although this is disappointing, those that have survived are both interesting and evocative. Whatever their ultimate fate, however, significant quantities of brick, timber and other structural or finishing elements must originally have been excavated, but cannot now contribute to a definitive interpretation of the form, constructional methods or finishes of the building. The disappearance of window glass fragments, which were originally retained, also closes a potentially useful line of enquiry. Nevertheless, the surviving fragments do provide some tantalising hints of what the building may have looked like, both inside and out.

■ *Late medieval floor tiles*

Six floor tile fragments in the archive could date as early as the 14th century, and were made no later than the beginning of the 16th century, providing valuable evidence for late medieval and early Tudor activity in the vicinity (Fig 63).[150] The tiles are green-glazed, some of which still remains, and are of Dutch origin. Pinholes can be seen in the corners of some examples, made during manufacture by the tile-maker to secure the tile in its wooden frame with a thin nail, to prevent shrinkage. A double pinhole resulted in one instance when the tile-maker missed his securing point the first time, so having to make a second attempt, which presumably was successful.

It is possible that these medieval tiles were reused from a local building, possibly the parish church, as they denote a relatively high status. They could perhaps have been used in the floor of the earliest (Phase 1) farmhouse, or perhaps even an earlier building on the same site, although no other evidence for such a structure has been uncovered in any of the available sources.

The things of everyday life

Fig 63: Fragments of Dutch green-glazed floor tiles, c 1300–1500

■ **Tin-glazed wall and floor tiles**

Six small tile fragments in tin-glazed earthenware were retained in the archive.[151] The earliest datable example is a fragment of floor tile, 16 mm thick, decorated in blue on white (Fig 64). This is almost certainly part of a polychrome tile, which could be of English (that is, London) manufacture (late 16th to mid 17th century) or Dutch (c 1560–1600).[152] Another fragment of a probable late 16th- to mid 17th-century tin-glazed floor tile is in too fragmentary a state to allow its overall thickness to be measured, or its design to be reconstructed. The surviving decoration consists of an animal head in yellow, outlined in blue, for which a parallel is hard to find. It seems very unlikely that fragments of tin-glazed tiles would have been discarded by the excavation team. If the tiles represent material discarded during one of the phases of development in the history of the building, rather than waste brought in as hardcore from elsewhere, then this may argue for the presence of an area of colourful, tiled flooring in the farmhouse in its earliest phase.

The remaining fragments all come from wall tiles. One of these has a landscape design painted in blue on white, but is too small for the overall scheme to be reconstructed, or to determine whether it is English or Dutch. A broad 18th-century date is given. A slightly larger fragment is decorated in blue on white with a manganese purple border (Fig 65). The main decoration shows a flower vase with

Fig 64: Fragment of tin-glazed earthenware floor tile, English or Dutch, late 16th to mid 17th century

Fig 65: Fragment of a London tin-glazed ware wall tile, dated to c 1740–60

birds on either side. This example can be attributed to London and dated between *c* 1740 and 1760.[153] Part of a tile with a mounted soldier painted in purple is a typical Dutch design, dated to *c* 1680–1750 (only the rear leg and most of the horse's tail have survived). Finally, part of a tile, 8 mm thick, and originally painted in blue on white with a landscape or Biblical scene and barred ox-head corner motifs, is of English or Dutch manufacture, dated to the late17th to 18th century. The presence of these tiles provides important clues to the appearance of the interior of the farmhouse in Phase 2, and they may well have been used in a fireplace, as was common at this period.

■ *Victorian tiles*

Fragments of six mid 19th-century Minton floor tiles were found in the archive, all coming from the same context. One of them has a very clear year mark for 1866 stamped on the reverse.[154] The use of the name 'MINTON', confirms the tile as made before 1873, the date at which the plural version 'MINTONS' came into use.[155] Five of the tiles have encaustic decoration, four of them in yellow on terracotta (Fig 66) and one with a black background (Fig 67).[156] These tiles are all more or less the same size, that is, 147–48 mm sq and 12.5 mm in thickness. Encaustic tiles are especially durable, their unique process of manufacture involving the pouring of coloured slips into deep moulded patterns. They are unglazed, but retain their colour over the years, and were decorated with a range of traditional and original designs, which many manufacturers sold through catalogues. This process of making inlaid tiles was perfected by Herbert Minton of Stoke-on-Trent, with medieval tiles providing a significant influence as part of the 19th-century Gothic Revival. These influences can clearly be seen in the tiles from Church End Farm. The tiles could be seen as part of a tiled floor with a design scheme incorporating a contrasting perimeter band and centre, and if they all date to the 1860s could have been introduced early on in William Frost Sweetland's occupation of Church End

Fig 66: Minton encaustic floor tile, mid 19th century

Fig 67: Minton encaustic floor tile, mid 19th century

House. They were perhaps laid at the time that the 'covered way' was constructed to the east of Church End Farm farmhouse, giving access between the yard and the gardens to the west of the 'new farmhouse'.

The sixth surviving Victorian tile from Church End Farm is of 'sandwich clay' construction, a process that originated in 1855.[157] It is block-printed in black and ochre on white, and is both slightly larger and thicker: 152 mm sq by 25 mm thick. A diamond-shaped registration mark on the underside is unclear, but could date it to 1871. The tile may have come from the conservatory floor. There is also one large fragment of a standard, unglazed, redware Platt floor tile, which probably dates from the second half of the 19th century.

■ Coins and tokens

Don Cooper

Coins have always been an invaluable dating tool for the archaeologist, precisely because they bear the date of issue, or the reign of the monarch under whom they were minted is well known historically. Twelve coins, two jettons, one bale seal and one token were recovered from the Church End Farm excavations. The following table is a list of the items in ascending date sequence, with their earliest and latest dates, the contexts in which they were found and the dates associated with the contexts without the coins (based mainly on pottery and clay pipes).[158]

Table 1: coins and jettons from Church End Farm

Find no.	Description	Date	Comment	Context	Context dates
E1	Elizabeth I – silver 6d	1566	'Liz Ab'	K	1640–1660
E2	Jetton – Wolf Lauffer, Nuremberg	1612–31	Image of military leader, turrets/castle background	L/M	1600–1700
E16	Jetton – Wolf Lauffer, Nuremberg	1612–31		SR	1660–1700
E3	Charles I – 1/4d	1625–49		N	1680–1700
E11	Charles I – 1/4d	1625–49	'CARO…'(LUS)	KS	1630–1680
E4	William and Mary – 1/2d	1689–94	'SEQUI….' 2 heads	M	1630–1700
E9	William III – groat?	1697		GU	1800–1880
E6	Queen Anne token	1702–14	'The foundation of our peace'	BG	1720–1740
E12	George I – 1/2d	1717–24		AH?	1720–1730
E10	George I – 1/2d	1719		IM	1740–1780
E14	George III – 1/4	1760–1820		NC	1760–1820
E8	George III – 1/2d	1773		DU	1773–1780
E15	George III – 1/2d	1799–1806		RH	1807–1850
E5	Communion token			M	1630–1700
E7	Farthing? 18th C.			CG	1740–1800
E13	Farthing-sized (unidentifiable)			VZ	No date

The original excavation diaries indicate that this list represents the total number of coins, jettons and tokens recovered. Even bearing in mind that the site was investigated before metal detectors were routinely used on archaeological sites, this is a relatively small number of finds. However, with the reigns of seven different monarchs represented covering almost 250 years, it more or less mirrors the life-cycle of Church End Farm. In some instances, the coin dates are earlier than the ceramic date range for the context in which they were found, but this is not unusual, given the degree of disturbance recorded on the site, and the ease with which small objects such as coins can become chronologically displaced. Coins can also remain in circulation as small change or even gaming counters long after the reign of the monarch for whom they were minted.

A worn 1566 silver sixpence from the reign of Elizabeth I, a relatively common coin, was found at a depth of 12 inches below the tiled floor on Site 1 (Fig 68). Other finds in the same context date to the mid 17th century and form part of a general layer of hardcore or ballast underneath and clearly predating the floor. The coin is the earliest closely datable artefact found on the site. There are very few other finds that can definitely be dated to the 16th century, and although it may hint at earlier

Fig 68: Elizabeth I silver sixpence, dated 1566, from the site of the farmhouse

Fig 69: Wolf Lauffer jetton, 1612–31, found on the site of the farmhouse

activity on the site, it could also have been retained long past its period of currency and then lost or deliberately discarded.

Two jettons of Wolf Lauffer of Nuremberg were also found on the site of the farmhouse (Fig 69). Both date to 1612–31 and come from 17th-century contexts, one of them probably deposited after *c* 1660. Jettons were originally made and used as reckoning counters in the calculation of accounts. They do not have a value as such, but are used on a reckoning table or cloth in the same way as the beads on an abacus. English jettons were no longer made in quantity after the late 14th century, after which they were imported from France and then from Nuremberg, which was the chief source of the jettons used in England from the mid 16th century. Some of those issued between *c* 1550 and 1630 are very common on excavations across the country, with Wolf Lauffer II one of a family associated with the production of jettons from 1554 to 1670. By *c* 1630, jettons were seldom used for reckoning any more in the large towns and cities, but continued to be made and circulated.[159] In a rural backwater such as Hendon in the 17th century, they could have been put to many uses by the occupants of the farmhouse, including reckoning, gaming counters, toys, or even small change. An English token, again from the site of the farmhouse (Site 1), dates from the short reign of Queen Anne, 1702–14. The legend reads 'The foundation of our peace', referring probably to the Church. A token of this kind would have been used in much the same way as the Wolf Lauffer jettons of 100 years earlier, for accounting or gaming, and as toys. The token was found in a context that also contained pottery dating to *c* 1720–40, so provides good confirmatory evidence.

Two Charles I farthings, a William and Mary halfpenny and a William III groat (fourpence) or possibly a sixpence span the 17th century. The other coins found on the site all date from the 18th to early 19th century. These include a George I farthing and a George II or III halfpenny, both from the site of The Paddock. No Victorian or later coins were found (or kept).

■ An ivory comb, toys, tools and knives

Don Cooper

The few other artefacts from Church End Farm that have survived include part of an ivory cigarette holder dating to the 20th century, an ivory knife handle, three ceramic beads from a necklace or

Fig 70: Ivory comb, probably 17th century in date

bracelet and various pieces of unidentifiable leather. Rather more interesting is part of a rectangular, double-edged, ivory comb with teeth of different sizes along each side (Fig 70). This is the common form of hair comb in use during the 17th and 18th centuries, made in various different materials (including horn, bone and tortoiseshell) and remaining popular with the less well-off into the 19th century.[160] Scratches on the fine tooth side show that it had been cleaned by its owner, perhaps with a pin or needle.[161]

Unfortunately, only six of the metal objects from Church End Farm have survived. The excavation diaries list between 175 and 200 objects, mostly nails and pins. The imprecision is due to entries such as 'various metal objects'. About 40 items were recorded as 'small finds' and given a unique number. These included six metal buttons; a thimble; 22 pins; pieces of window leading; one spoon; a large, two-pronged fork; three barrel hoops; three metal rings; parts of door hinges and two metal buckles. None of these can now be located.

The surviving metal finds present an eclectic mix.[162] They include two children's toys, the earlier of which probably dates to the 19th century, a period that is not so well represented in the material recovered from the site. It is in the form of a hollow trumpet in thin sheet metal (tin), and in rather poor condition. The presence of a valve on the instrument, places it after their introduction in the early 19th century. The other metal toy is a lead tank of the kind developed during World War 1. Some of the porcelain limbs of a small doll probably date to the late 19th or early 20th century, presenting a gentler aspect of children at play.

Apart from the early 20th-century toy tank, the remaining metal finds are mostly in poor condition. Part of a pick with a long, curved tip and short socket is in a badly corroded state. It is not quite right for an ice pick, although it appears to have been made for specialised use and probably dates to the 19th century.[163] A chisel and parts of two corroded knives are the only other finds that have survived. Whether or not the knives were made for the table or for other purposes is altogether uncertain. An unstratified brass button of a kind known as a 'ball button' can be identified with the Buckinghamshire Yoemanry.[164] Overall, there are too few metal objects to add very much to the story of Church End Farm. They give us the briefest glimpses of the farmstead's children at play, and of the working man's tools.

■ Animal bones: daily food and wildlife

Geraldine Missig

Archaeologists look to artefacts to answer questions about the site on which they were found, and each class of artefact plays its unique part in weaving the overall tapestry. It is no different with animal bone, which contributes to the picture by providing clues to the past relationships between man and the animals that occupied his environment.

What part did the animals play in man's life and economy? Did they have a key part in agricultural endeavours, providing traction and/or milk or meat, or were they used in industrial activities again, providing power or perhaps just raw materials (for example, for glue production or leather working)? Could their bones simply be the remains of daily food discarded after use, but nevertheless revealing to subsequent generations the diet and social status of the consumers?

Bone draws other pictures as well. A buried pet attests to man's domestication and humanity, whilst the bones of animals which exist alongside man but mainly outside his use, let alone his awareness, such as the rat, the mouse or the mole, remind us of the different worlds which exist independently of man. By looking at the bone remains from Church End Farm it is hoped to establish the patterns that reveal the nature of its inhabitants' relationship with their animals.

■ Historical background

The original construction and development of Church End Farm probably coincides with the rapid expansion of London's population in the early 17th century. This necessitated the development of new methods of providing food for its inhabitants; consequently, agriculture became more organised and specialised. New metropolitan meat markets were created to handle the volume of animals needed,[165] and farmers in the areas surrounding London specialised in different products.

With cattle, the business was divided into dairy farming, veal production and beef farming. The latter was the least profitable form for farmers close to London. A cattle trade network therefore developed whereby it was more economic for animals to be born and raised in the more distant parts of Britain, sold for final fattening in the fields of the farmers close to London and moved thence to the meat markets.[166]

In order to maintain levels of milk production, dairy cows need to calve annually. The infant females who were not needed to replenish the dairy herd and the infant males who were surplus to requirement[167] were sold to graziers who fattened them until 10 to 12 weeks, when they would be sold to the butchers for veal. Some dairies raised their own infants until this age, whereupon they would be sold directly to the butchers.[168] If Church End Farm were involved in these kinds of activities it would be expected that the bone remains would contain some evidence of it.

■ The bones

A total of 565 contexts were recorded on the combined sites of Church End Farm, of which 94 or 17% contained bone. Considering The Paddock's close association with animals, it produced disappointingly few bone remains. The excavators questioned whether Site 2 had acid soil, but there is no record that it was tested. In all, 28 bones, including teeth, were found in the Barn (Site 3), but the highest concentration came from the farmhouse site, with Trenches 17, 18 and 20 yielding the most bones.

The bones of an assemblage can be counted in different ways but the simplest, most basic and immediate is to count the number of identified specimens or NISP. Each fragment that can be identified as to animal and anatomical part is counted, even if incomplete. Only seven fragments and nine teeth could not be identified, and 43 fragments were unstratified, leaving a total of 213 NISP for the combined sites, of which 43 were unstratified. Animals contain different numbers of bones, thus influencing the representation of species and by its very nature the NISP count favours the larger species. Their bigger, denser bones have a better chance of survival after death and are therefore more likely to leave fragments that can be identified. There is also a bias towards the larger animals on the site because no sieving was carried out during excavation, which would have increased the number of smaller bones retrieved.

The NISP count deals merely with numbers of fragments, which does not give any idea of the number of animals those pieces represent. This can be overcome by determining the minimum number of individuals (MNI) necessary to account for the amount of a skeletal part present. In seeking to organize anonymous fragments into animals, the MNI count does not necessarily describe the actual number of individuals; it only represents the smallest number possible.

■ *The species*

The species identified at Church End Farm are those that would be expected in an agricultural setting. Fragments of cattle bones are most numerous, at 36% of the sample, and sheep/goat the next most common, at 24%, with pig a poor third at 16%. It is difficult to distinguish between the bones of sheep and goats, as they are morphologically quite similar, although some bones display diagnostic features that allow closer identification. Only six useable diagnostic bones were identified at Church End Farm, of which five belonged to sheep and one to goat. The remaining bones are simply recorded as sheep/goat. Horse bones comprise only 3% of the entire sample, while fragments of the small bones of the rat and mole are more frequent at 7% and 4% respectively. The absence of any evidence of dogs or cats is surprising, as is the scarcity of bird bones.

■ *Condition of the bones*

Although the sample of bones is small, there is a clear pattern in their condition. It would be expected that the bones of the largest species, cattle, would fare better than the smaller, the rat, the mole and even the sheep/goat. However, although more frequent, they are in the poorest condition, with more than half the sample represented by small fragments and only 10% consisting of whole bones. The sheep/goat bones are less frequent, possibly because they are smaller, less dense and therefore more easily obliterated, but they are also less fragmented, with 24% of the sample consisting of whole bones. The rat and mole bones present a different picture, as they are complete or very nearly so. The reason, of course, lies in the final use of the animal. Overall, 73% of the cattle and 52% of the sheep/goat bones show evidence of butchery whilst the rat and the mole, unsurprisingly, show none.

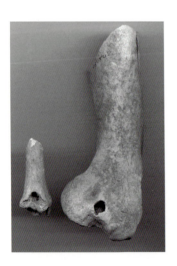

Fig 71: Cattle and sheep/goat bones showing small holes, possibly made for the extraction of marrow

There was evidence throughout the assemblage of dog and rodent gnawing; even 36% of the rat bones show signs of rodent gnawing, although it did not affect their condition. A relatively high proportion of the cattle bones (37%) showed signs of erosion and weathering and 40% of them had been gnawed by dogs, suggesting that they had been lying on the surface for some time before burial. Longer exposure to air and wear would have increased the rate of deterioration, although their condition may also have resulted from heating. Small, irregular, round holes of varying sizes can be found in the distal ends of the cattle humeri, metatarsal and sheep/goat's tibia and in the proximal ends of the cattle radius, femur and first phalanx (Fig 71). One possible suggestion for the holes is that they are a consequence of being swung on a meat hook; another is that they were made to allow the extraction of marrow, fat and oil when the bones were boiled in water.[169]

There are other instances in the past of bones being heated.

Boiling the foot bones of cattle in vats of water produces high quality yellow oil called neatsfoot oil, which was used for dressing leather products.[170] Calves' foot jelly was prepared in the home by stewing calves feet.[171] Even today stock is made by simmering bones in water for about four hours together with other ingredients, including, no doubt, the corrosive agent, salt. Bones have always been an important ingredient in some soups. The scapula, humerus, radius and tibia form those fattier, less tender cuts of meat that are better suited to long, slow cooking, often in liquid. *The Joy of Cooking (1953)* exhorts its reader 'You pay for bones, so utilise their values' and adds that 'Bones are not without their advantages for flavour and especially for calcium, which can be extracted to advantage in recipes calling for vinegar or wine soaking and cooking'.

■ Ageing cattle, sheep/goat and pig

The age of an animal can be ascertained by the state of fusion of its bones. As a bone is growing its proximal and distal epiphyses are loosely attached with cartilage to enable bone growth to occur. When full growth is achieved the epiphyses become firmly attached to the shaft and the bone is said to be fused. This occurs at different rates for different bones and can even be at different times for the two ends of the same bone. Bones can be early, mid or late fusing, and these categories are the same for cattle, sheep/goat and pig. Each bone has an age range within which the bone fuses. However, there are not many unfused bones of cattle, sheep/goat and pig in the assemblage. Does this accurately reflect the ages of the animal population that lived at Church End Farm? Would the softer, more fragile and porous bones of the immature animal survive where there was so high a degree of fragmentation, and where the cattle bones were in such poor condition, with evidence of much dog activity? Would there have been more found if there had been sieving? Or were there were few young animals, as the figures suggest?

Another means of ageing cattle, sheep/goat and, to some extent, pig, is through the sequence of eruption of their teeth. However, once teeth are erupted, this method is no longer applicable and methods of ageing on the basis of wear stages of teeth have been developed based on studies of modern animals. It is not a new concept; the anterior teeth of animals were looked at by prospective purchasers and the phrase 'Never look a gift horse in the mouth' still survives. The ages are given as ranges, based on the wear relationships in the animal's mandible (jawbone), since this is usually one of the best-preserved bones on a site. It does not contain much meat, so is not attractive to animals, which are also deterred by the teeth, not wanting to damage their own on such a hard surface.[172]Despite this, five of the mandible fragments of the Church End Farm site display marks of animal gnawing. The sample again suffers from its small size, but analysis shows that there were differences of ages within the group. Of the three cattle mandibles, one is between 3 and 6 months, one between 3 and 6 years and the other in the 6 to 8 year range. Outside a wear relationship, but still capable of being broadly categorised are nine loose upper and lower teeth. Of these, three are very young, one young and five are mature. Apart from these teeth, there is no osteological evidence in the assemblage of young cattle. The ages of sheep/goat teeth were more difficult to ascertain, as many of the diagnostic teeth were missing. There were no really young animals, which agrees with the bone fusion evidence, but the teeth show a spread of ages between about 1-10 years.

Four pig mandibles range in age from under 12 months to 2-3 years old. Other fragments were from younger individuals: one from Site 3 came from an individual under 6 months and another from

Site 1 came from an animal less than 12 months. The wear on one loose lower tooth from Site 1 indicates that the owner had been older than 12 to 16 months. The cattle, sheep/goat and pig teeth hint at a larger number of individuals than the bone MNI count does and they suggest the presence of more young animals than does the evidence from the unfused bone.

■ Representation of skeletal elements

'Any variability in the relative frequencies of anatomical parts among archaeological sites must derive from the dynamics of their use'.[173] If Church End Farm was a place of animal slaughter, there would be a sizeable quantity of bone and waste bone such as skull or skull fragments and all three types of phalanges (toe bones). Similarly, if industrial activity such as tanning or making tallow took place there, a surplus of a limited variety of used bone would be expected. The bone assemblage of the five most frequently found species is not large and does not represent a wide or random variety of parts. It does, however, show a preponderance of cattle meat-bearing bones (the limb bones, the scapula, pelvis, vertebrae and ribs). Sheep/goat is less frequent, with tibias (shanks) and vertebrae (chops) the most common bones. Pigs are even less frequent and are represented by metatarsals (trotters) and ribs.

The higher the quantity of meat, marrow and grease a particular skeletal element possesses, the more desirable the part, with more effort and investment put into obtaining it. The presence of such bones on a site provides a guide to the social status of the consumers. On this basis, the bones of Church End Farm can be considered high value meat bones.[174] The cattle bones are highly fragmented and heavily butchered, with few whole bones remaining. To a lesser degree so are the sheep/goat and pig bones. In all these respects the animal bone assemblage fits into the category of food waste.[175] Furthermore, many bones display features of severe erosion, possibly as result of heating and several exhibit small, round holes, possibly as a consequence of meat processing or marrow extraction.

■ The other species

Birds were poorly represented. To aid them in flight, bird bones are lighter and more hollow than mammal bones.[176] They are, therefore, less likely to survive. However, farm work is laborious and requires a lot of energy, which may be better provided by a food of higher calorific value and fat content than bird. The few bones of domestic fowl (all from late 17th- to mid 18th-century contexts) and goose (three out of four bones from 17th- to 18th-century levels) were all wing bones. These carry little meat and could be removed before serving, particularly if damaged.[177]

There were also very few fish bones. Six haddock vertebrae (all late 17th- to mid 18th-century) were found in a deep layer in the trench in the barn. A species related to cod, haddock was fished in the waters of the North Atlantic and traded at the ports of Southampton, Yarmouth or Yorkshire. Before the advent of refrigeration such fish could be transported long distances only after some form of preservation, such as pickling, salting or salting and drying.[178]

The bones of a number of small animals – rat, mole, hare and rabbit – were in very good condition. Their bones, if not whole, are more than 75% complete and not eroded like the cattle bones. There is no evidence from the bones that the rabbits (two bones) or hare (four bones) finished up on the dining table. Although the rabbit is a burrowing animal and the bones were found in shallow layers, there is no record of their coming from loose earth or a burrow system. If an animal died in a burrow, more skeletal evidence would be expected, although this might have been forthcoming if the soil had been sieved.[179]

It is not surprising that on a farm with easy access to food, the rat was as well represented as it was. Fourteen rat bones were found, including one skull. The bones were evenly distributed between the barn and the old farmhouse, with the highest concentration (six bones) dating to the late 17th to mid 18th century. The skull was identified as that of a brown rat, which was only introduced into Britain in the late 17th to early 18th century, fitting in closely with its dating at Church End Farm.[180] Its habitat is different from that of the black rat, in that it lives closer to the ground and can develop tunnel systems. However, if living in the same area, the brown rat will dominate and drive out the black.[181] Unfortunately, the earlier rat bones from the site do not have any diagnostic features to distinguish brown from black.

The skulls and related small bones of two moles were found beneath the tiled floor of the old farmhouse in Site 1, all dated to the late 17th to mid 18th century (Fig 72). This, however, may not have been where they lived or died. There was no record of any burrow network and moles are solitary

Fig 72: One of two mole skulls found underneath the tiled floor on Site 1

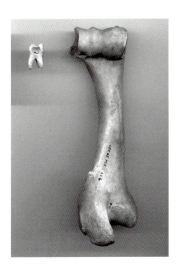

Fig 73: Human upper third molar from below the tiled floor (left) and sheep humerus showing signs of 'penning elbow' (right)

creatures, with usually only one occupying a particular tunnel system at any one time.[182] There was no evidence of dogs or cats in the sample and only one horse bone and five teeth. This suggests that the remains of these common agricultural animals were treated differently from those used for food on the site.

■ *Pathology*

A sheep humerus found in the barn, and dating to the early 19th century, shows the telltale overgrowth of bone associated with 'penning elbow' (Fig 73, right). This was thought to be a condition resulting from animals being penned together, although it has also been found in animals that could not have been penned.[183]

A human upper third molar was found in an early to mid 17th-century context underneath the tiled floor (Fig 73, left). The third molar appears between the ages of 17 and 25, if it appears at all.[184] The occlusal surface of the tooth shows little wear and no caries. However, there is a very large hole on the side of the tooth where it sat beside its neighbour. The hole stretches from the top of the tooth down into the root and shows no sign of attempted dental repair. The tooth also suffers from layers of plaque on the inside of the root surfaces, which would only be possible if that area of the gum was diseased and recessed, so exposing the root. The end tip of one of the roots is broken, but still covered with calculus.

■ Conclusion

The Church End Farm excavations produced a sample of bones from an agricultural site that appears to have developed in the early to mid 17th century, close to London, and which enjoyed continuous agricultural use. The excavated bones came mostly from the farmhouse area and were therefore more likely to represent household waste. Although there were trenches in The Paddock, no evidence was found for the dwelling shown on its margin in Crow's map of 1754. Further trenches in the working areas of the farm might have provided bone illustrating a different use.

How representative is the small number of bones collected? The disparity between the number of cattle fragments and sheep/goat and pig fragments retrieved raises questions about how accurately they reflect the relative proportions originally present, especially since no sieving was carried out. The cattle fragments are in poor condition and the number of teeth found suggests a greater animal population with a larger number of younger animals than were indicated by bone only. There is, however, a clear pattern of butchery and dog gnawing of cattle bones and to a lesser degree the sheep/goat, although the pig bones are too few to extract clear patterns.

Bearing these caveats in mind, the bones from Church End Farm, apart from the small animals, appear to represent the remains of food consumption, initially by humans and secondarily by dogs, rather than the by-products of agricultural or industrial activity. By far the largest concentration of bones comes from building Phase 1 (early to mid 17th century) with half as many again from Phase 2 (late 17th to mid 18th century). The numbers from late 18th- to 20th-century contexts are so low as to indicate a different type of deposition. This general pattern can also be seen in the other finds. A possible explanation is that most of the bones were included in fills used as hardcore in the construction of the farmhouse. This fits in with an early to mid 17th-century date for the construction of the farmhouse, although the animal bones could also conceivably include domestic waste of Church End Farm's neighbours.

In any event, the cuts of meat represented by the bones and the small holes in the distal ends of some bones suggest that a wide range of cooking methods were utilised. The seemingly more numerous cattle bones may imply that beef was favoured over sheep or pig. The proportion of high value cuts of meat (limbs) in the sample soundly outweighs the low value cuts (neck, skull and toes). This suggests that the inhabitants of Church End Farm ate well, although rural agricultural communities probably had easier access to a better quality of food in relation to their economic status than urban dwellers.

The last Hendon farm
CHAPTER 6:

FUTURE WORK

While the project team has encountered some difficulties in its interrogation of the site records and data, the broad excavation record has provided hard facts and the basis, after finds recording, for analysing finds data in ways not open to the original excavation team. This analysis has brought a greater understanding of Church End Farm as a place where successive generations lived and worked, adding information and new insights to the perspectives already provided by the earlier studies generated by the excavation. The greater part of the finds evidence is concerned with the ceramics and animal bones, since other categories of finds were either sparsely represented or were lost after the end of the excavation. The surviving evidence does, however, illustrate something of the richness of the site, and has greatly enhanced the significance of the information available from the excavation photography and the documentary research, enabling a more rounded picture of this substantial and important farmstead to emerge. For substantial and important it undoubtedly was, in the context of the known development of Church End in the 17th and 18th century. The evidence considered has allowed a reasonably confident dating of the building to no later than 1650, providing a firm basis for further research and study.

Both the archaeology and documentary sources give a picture of continuous occupation of a single site (and probably a single building) over three centuries. The excavated material remains convey a trenchant picture of particular standards of comfort and living, which can now be meaningfully compared with other local farmhouse and farmstead sites. The finds alone support the social and working dignity of this lost farm and farm house, suggesting, in Church End Farm farmhouse, a building as evocative in its own way of Hendon's past as that magnificent standing structure, Church Farm farmhouse (Church End Farmhouse Museum), its old neighbour across Hall Lane. Its loss is great. The merits of the excavation team and those who inspired and encouraged their activities are therefore all the greater for having given us this opportunity to see and learn afresh and anew. Ted Sammes' own commitment to this excavation and this history is vindicated

The last Hendon farm
APPENDICES

APPENDIX 1: DOCUMENTARY SOURCES FOR CHURCH END FARM FARMHOUSE AND FARM

Christopher Willey

The following is a brief resumé of some of the primary and secondary documentary sources that have provided information and a 'context' for the building history and archaeology.

■ Primary sources

Documentary sources, principally held within the London Borough of Barnet Local History Archive (LBBLSA), are given in the appropriate footnotes. Some additional primary material was obtained and consulted by Ian Robertson and Ted Sammes in the early 1960s, and other documentary work was carried out by Sammes in the later 1960s in support of excavations at Peacocks Yard, Mount Pleasant and The Retreat, centrally sited at Church End. Where relevant to this study, his transcripts of primary documents have been treated as primary sources, since they bear references, even though, in some cases, the holding archive has changed since the 1960s or the precise source is unclear. Their use in this way may be a little irregular, but seems in the spirit of a report concerned in part with the 'archaeology of archaeology'. Sammes' own references are given in full wherever possible. His approach as a documentary researcher generally gives considerable confidence.

National Census returns for Church End were consulted for 1841, 1851, 1881 and 1891. While interesting, the difficulty of locating residence to a particular building within the Church End Farm complex limited the value of information gained.

■ Secondary sources

Walford (1883) provides some hints on the largely unprovenanced medieval history of Church End and Hendon circulating in his time. The question of a link between Church End, and in particular Church End Farm, with a hall or hall farm occupied by the Abbot of Westminster's bailiff is considered in a paper by Pamela Taylor delivered at a HADAS seminar in May 1993. A copy of this was kindly provided to the project team. Pigot and Co.'s Directory for Middlesex and the Towns and Villages within 12 miles of London (1826, 450) and Kelly's Directory for Middlesex (1851, 532-533) were consulted for possible trade or occupancy details for Church End Farm, but without positive result.

■ Mapping

The following mapping is seen as of particular interest. All the maps were consulted at the London Borough of Barnet Local History Archive.

Appendices

- ### Crow's map, 1754

This usefully includes field names, making it easier to delineate the physical boundaries of Church End Farm as a 'farm let' in the mid 18th century, relative to other Church End farms and holdings. This map provides, with the successive Indentures of Lease for the farm lets and the Catalogue of Sale mapping referred to below, a first 'photograph' for the historic Church End Farm and its probable 17th- and early 18th-century precursors, to which the excavated finds and other evidence point.

- ### Catalogue of Sale for the Parish Lands of Hendon 1754/6, mapping

This provides careful lists of tenants by holding, field size, and agricultural use for the Manor of Hendon, with mapping of holdings, structures, and features at scales varying from 10 to 40 poles to the inch. A longhand note on the front of one of the copies confirms that Thomas Nicholl, as tenant of Church End Farm, was both farmer and bricklayer.

- ### Messeder's 'A plan of the Manor & Parish of Hendon, 1783 ~ a copy of the 1754 original

The scale of this map permits a more effective 'bird's eye' view of the farm holdings of interest, but it essentially corresponds in details to Crow's Map.

- ### Rankin and Johnson's estate plan for Church End Farm 'estate' surveyed by J Prickett, 1789

This is probably the most detailed mapping of Church End Farm produced in the 18th century, giving some clues on the possible building history of the 18th century splayed bay, and suggestive detail on the offices, areas, gardens, ponds and orchard in and around the house and immediate environs.

- ### Cook's Map 1796, with associated Field Book

This is exceptionally useful in providing a social and ownership locus for Church End Farm and its immediate environs at the end of the 18th century. It also confirms or guides interpretation of building detail and the locations of and possible relationship between structures shown as in different ownership. Unfortunately, the scale of the mapping leads to occasional ambiguity in the interpretation of the numerical codes for properties listed in the Reference sheets. The number codes do not go far enough in respect of the Church End Farm 'steading' to cast light on any sub-division of occupation.

- ### Walter Johnson's estate maps

From the late 19th and early 20th century, these confirm the continuity of the physical 'entity' of Church End Farm, but record railway and aeronautical incursions.

- OS sequence, 25 inches to 1 mile (latterly 1:2500), editions of 1863, 1914, 1936 and 1956, for Hendon village.

The references in the text to the Ordnance Survey are to this series.

APPENDIX 2: CHRONOLOGICAL LIST OF PROBABLE OCCUPANTS OF CHURCH END FARM, 1741 TO 1940

Date	Name of tenant/occupant	Occupation*	Source
1741	Thomas Nicholl	Farmer and bricklayer/maker	Catalogue of Sale 1754/6, and 'A Particular and Valuation of the Manor of Hendon in the County of Middlesex, March 1753' LBBLSA
1791	William Geeves Jnr	Farmer	Bischoff, B1/25, LBBLSA
1812	Edward Nicholl the younger	Hay salesman, dealer and chapman**	Bischoff, B1/33, 135, 137, LBBLSA
1827	William Bignall	Farmer	Bischoff, B1/33, LBBLSA
1840	William Wiggins – *house 1840, farm 1841*	Farmer and126, LBBLSA	Bischoff, B1/39
1850	William Frost Sweetland – *Mr Sweetland held the farm let but occupied Church Farm House from 1853*	Dairyman farmer, and condensed milk pioneer	Bischoff, B1/137, LBBLSA
1881	William Horton – *assumed part only. Cottage in farmyard given as uninhabited*	Agricultural labourer	1881 National Census, PRO RG11/Piece 1366
1882	Kirby – *possibly here occupier of the larger part of a sub-divided farmhouse, with another unnamed occupier in 'cottage'*	Hendon, 1350/4, LBBLSA	General District Rate for
1887	Edward McMillan/William Orton – *possibly occupying two parts of a sub-divided farmhouse*	McMillan given later as a carman. Orton probably in error for Horton, previously given as agricultural labourer	General District Rate for Hendon, 1350/1, LBBLSA
1888	Edward McMillan – *occupying 'cottage and garden'*	?Carman	General District Rate for Hendon, 1350/1, LBBLSA
	William Horton – *occupying 'cottage'*	Previously given as agricultural labourer	Hinge now seems to be operating the farm

Appendices

Date	Name of tenant/occupant	Occupation*	Source
1889	Edward McMillan – *occupying 'cottage and garden'*	?Carman	General District Rate for Hendon, 1350/3, LBBLSA
	Charles Ball - *occupying 'cottage'*	Given later as farm labourer	
1891	Charles Ball – 3 rooms –*possibly occupying new accommodation to east of covered entrance way from yard to Church Farm House*	Farm labourer	1891 National Census, PRO RG12/1049
	Frank Sweetland, his sister Ellen, a cook and housemaid – occupying more than 5 rooms	Dairyman manager	*The reading linking Charles Ball to new accommodation is based on the apparent increase in habitations listed in the National Census between 1881 and 1891. Edward McMillan is interpreted as living in the two western bays of the farmhouse, and Frank Sweetland's household in the two larger eastern bays.*
	Edward McMillan – occupying 4 rooms	Carman***	

* The occupation given is that of the head of the household.

** A man who buys and sells; a merchant, a dealer – Lesley Brown, ed., *The New Shorter Oxford English Dictionary*, (Clarendon Press, 1993).

*** A driver of a van etc., a carrier – *Ibid*. The longhand entry is a little difficult to read but seems to exclude a reading as 'cowman'.

The last Hendon farm
BIBLIOGRAPHY & NOTES

BIBLIOGRAPHY

Abrams, F W H 1982, *The Kempes of Hendon and Church Farm House –Transactions No. 2 (New Series)*, Mill Hill and Hendon Historical Society

Addy, S O 1975, *The evolution of the English house, revised and enlarged from the author's notes by J Summerson, Reprint of 2nd Ed (1933)*, E P Publishing Ltd, British Book Centre, Inc

Armitage, P 1978, 'Hertfordshire cattle and London meat markets in the 17th and 18th centuries', *London Archaeol* 3, 217–223

Armitage, P, West, B and Steadman, K 1984, 'New evidence of black rat in Roman London', *London Archaeol* 4, 375–382

Atkinson, D R and Oswald, A 1969, 'London clay tobacco pipes', *J British Archaeol Assoc* 32, 171–227

Atkinson, D R 1975, *Tobacco pipes of Broseley, Shropshire*, Saffron Walden

Atterbury, P and Batkin, M 1999, *The dictionary of Minton*, Antique Collectors' Club

Ayto, E G 1979, *Clay tobacco pipes*, Shire Album 37

Barber, B and Thomas, C 2002, *The London Charterhouse*, MoLAS Monograph 10

Barnard, E A B 1948, 'Sparrows and sparrow pots', *Trans Worcestershire Archaeol Soc* 25, 50–59

Barlowe, F 1687, *Aesop's fables*, London: H Hills Jun

Betts, I M 2002, *Medieval 'Westminster' floor tiles*, MoLAS Monograph 11

BGS 1993, *British Geological Survey, North London, England and Wales Sheet 256, Solid and Drift Geology 1:50 000*

Binford, L R 1978, 'Nunamiut ethnoarchaeology', cited in Lyman, 1994, 225

Braun, H 1962, *Old English houses*, Faber and Faber

Brears, P C D 1974, *The collector's book of English country pottery*, London: David and Charles

Brett-James, N G 1932, *The story of Hendon - manor and parish*, Warden and Co.

Brown, R J 1982, *English farmhouses*, Robert Hale Ltd

Brunskill, R W 1971, *Illustrated handbook of vernacular architecture*, Faber and Faber

Brunskill, R W 1987, *Traditional farm buildings of Britain*, Victor Gollancz, in association with Peter Crawley, 1987

Brunskill, R W 1997, *Brick building in Britain*, Victor Gollancz, in assoc with Peter Crawley

Brunskill, R W 2000, *Vernacular architecture ~ an illustrated handbook*, Faber and Faber

Brunskill, R W and Clifton-Taylor, A 1977, *English brickwork*, Ward Lock

Butler, S 1775, *Hudibras*, London

Cave, L F 1981, *The smaller English house – its history and development*, Robert Hale

Cherry, B and Pevsner, N 1983, *The buildings of England, London 2: South*, Penguin Books

Cherry, B and Pevsner, N 1991, *The buildings of England, London 3: North West*, Penguin Books

Cherry, B and Pevsner, N 1998, *The buildings of England, London 4: North*, Penguin Books

Christianson, C P 2002, 'Tools from the medieval garden', *The London Gardener* 7, 17-21

Clark, J F M 2000, 'The Irishmen of birds' *History Today*, October 2000

Cohen, A and Serjeantson, D 1996, *A manual for the identification of bird bones from archaeological sites*, London: Archetype

Corporation of London Records Office (CLRO), *Manuscript of Bridge House Accounts, Weekly Payments, 2nd ser, vol 2, 1516-1528*, folio 377r

Coy, J 1989, 'The provision of fowl and fish for towns', in Serjeantson and Waldron

Divers, D 2004, 'Excavations at Deptford on the site of the East India Company dockyards and the Trinity House almshouses, London', *Post-medieval Archaeol* 38 part 1, 17–132

Evans, G E 1970, *Where beards wag all: the relevance of the oral tradition*, London: Faber and Faber

Fleming, J, Honour, H, Pevsner, N 1972, *A dictionary of architecture*, Penguin Books, 2nd edn

Fletcher, V 1968, *Chimney pots and stacks – an introduction to their history, variety and identification*, Centaur Press

Fowler, P 1983, *Farms in England – prehistoric to present*, Royal Commission on Historical Monuments England, HMSO

Gaimster, D 1997, *German stoneware 1200-1900*, London: British Museum Press

Garner, F H and Archer, M 1972, *English delftware*, London: Faber and Faber

Harris, R 1993, *Discovering timber-framed buildings*, Shire Publications, 3rd edn

Harvey, N 1970, *A history of farm buildings in England and Wales*, David and Charles

Hillson, S 1986, *Teeth*, Cambridge Manual in Archaeology, Cambridge University Press

Horne, J 1989, *English tinglazed tiles*, London: Jonathan Horne Publications

Hughes, M J 2003, *Report on the analysis of 31 birdpots by inductively-coupled plasma atomic emission spectrometric analysis (ICP-AES)*, unpubl report

Hurst, J G, Neal, D S and van Beuningen, H J E 1986, *Pottery produced and traded in north-west Europe 1350–1650*, Rotterdam Papers 6

Jones, J 1995, *Minton*, Shire Album 279

Klinge, E 1996, *German stoneware*, Rijksmuseum Amsterdam

Korf, D 1981, *Nederlandse majolica*, De Haan: Haarlem

Lawrence, M J and Brown, R W 1973, *Mammals of Britain; their tracks, trails and signs*, London: Blandford Press

Legge, A J 1981, 'The agricultural economy', in R J Mercer (ed), *Grimes Graves, Norfolk: excavations 1971-1972*, DOE Research Rep 11, London: HMSO, 79–117

Legge, A J 1992, 'Animals, environment and the Bronze Age economy', in *Excavations at Grimes Graves, Norfolk 1972-1976*, Fascicule 4, Part A: The Faunal Remains, London: British Museum

Press, 15–42

Lemmen, H van 1979, *Tiles – a collector's guide*, Souvenir Press

Lemmen, H van 2000, *Victorian tiles*, Shire Album 67

Lloyd, N 1925, *A history of English brickwork*, Antique Collectors' Club, 1983 facsimile reprint of 1925 edn

Lockett, T A 1979, *Collecting Victorian tiles*, Antique Collectors' Club

London Borough of Barnet Library Services 1972, *Church Farm House*, LB Barnet, New Edn

Loudon, J C 1842, *An encyclopaedia of cottage, farm, and villa architecture and furniture*, London: Longman, Brown, Green, and Longmans

Lynch, G 1994, *Brickwork – history, technology and practice, volume 1*, Donhead

McIntyre, S 1973, The mineral water trade in the 18th century, *J Transport History*, 2

Morris, J (ed/trans) 1975, Domesday Book 11 Middlesex, Chichester: Phillimore

MPRG 1998, *A guide to the classification of medieval ceramic forms*, Medieval Pottery Research Group

Noel Hume, I 1961, The glass wine bottle in colonial Virginia, *J Glass Studies* 3

Noel Hume, I 1969, *A guide to artifacts of colonial America*, Philadelphia: University of Pennsylvania Press

Notes and Queries, 6th ser, Vol 4, 1881, Various correspondents' comments on birdpots, Oxford: Oxford University Press

Oswald, A, 1975 *Clay pipes for the archaeologist*, BAR 14, Oxford

Payne, S 1972a, 'Partial recovery and sample bias: the results of some sieving experiments', in E S Higgs (ed), *Papers in economic history*, Cambridge University Press, 49–64

Payne, S 1972b, 'On the interpretation of bone samples from archaeological sites', in Higgs 1972, 65–81

Pearce, J 1992, *Border wares: post-medieval pottery in London, 1500–1700, volume 1*, London: HMSO

Penoyre, J and J 1978, *Houses in the landscape – a regional study of vernacular building styles in England and Wales*, Faber and Faber

Peters, J E C 1981, *Discovering traditional farm buildings*, Shire Publications

Pluis, J 1997, *The Dutch tile: designs and names*

Porter, R 1994, *London: a social history*, Hamish Hamilton

Ramsey, S C and Harvey, J D M 1972, Small *Georgian houses and their details 1750–1820*, (reprint by The Architectural Press of *Small houses of the late Georgian period, volumes I and II*, Crane, Rusack, 1919 and 1923

Rennie, J 1833, *Ornithological dictionary of British birds, by Colonel G Montagu*, London: W S Orr and W Smith

Robertson, I 1961, *Interim report on the excavations at Church End Farm, Hendon*, unpubl

Robertson, I 1962, *Interim report on the excavations at Church End Farm, Hendon*, unpubl

Rombauer, I and Rombauer-Becker, M 1953, *The joy of cooking*, New York: The Bobbs-Merrill

Company

Sammes, E 1986, *Pinning down the past – finds from a Hendon dig*, HADAS

Saul, S B 1969, *The myth of the Great Depression 1873-1896*, Studies in Economic History, M W Flinn (ed), Macmillan Student Editions

Serjeantson, D and Waldron, T (eds), *Diet and crafts in towns*, BAR British Ser 199

Serjeantson, D, Waldron, T and McCracken, S 1986, 'Veal and calfskin in eighteenth century Kingston', *London Archaeol* 5, 227–232

Stephenson, R 1991, 'Post-medieval ceramic bird pots from excavations in Greater London' *London Archaeol* 6 (12), 320–21

Summers-Smith, J D 1963, *The house sparrow*, London: Collins

Summerson, J 1962, *Georgian London – an architectural study*, Praeger edn (1970) of Penguin Books revised edn

Taylor, P (ed) 1989, *A place in time*, HADAS

Taylor, P 1993, unpubl paper for HADAS on the history of Church End

VCH 1976, *A history of the county of Middlesex, vol 5: the Victoria History of the Counties of England*, (ed R B Pugh), University of London Institute of Historical Research

Walford, E 1883, *The story of Greater London part I – West and North*, BAS Printers

Webb, C R 1996, *London apprentices vol 2 – Tylers' and Bricklayers' Company 1612–44 and 1668–1800*, Soc Geanealogists

Westman, A, Tyers, I, Jones, H 2001, *The Stables 7a – 7b Davies Lane Leytonstone, a standing building survey report commissioned by London Borough of Waltham Forest*, MoLAS unpubl rep

Woodforde, J 1983, *Farm buildings in England and Wales*, Routledge and Kegan Paul

END NOTES

[1] Morris 1975.

[2] Terry Smith (Museum of London Specialist Services) pers. comm.

[3] BGS Sheet 256, 1993.

[4] Taylor 1989, Fig 1.2.

[5] Bischoff papers, London Borough of Barnet Local History Archive (LBBLSA), B1/135: an agreement between B F Johnson and E C Nicoll.

[6] Peters 1981, 7.

[7] *Ibid*, 7 and Harvey 1970, 78-79.

[8] This plan is held in LBBLSA, Bischoff papers.

[9] Harvey 1970, 76.

[10] This can be seen in the 1863 25 inches to 1 mile and equivalent later series Ordnance Survey mapping. See Harvey 1970, 76 and 101-102 (note).

[11] These are perpetuated, in the case of Church End Farm, by successive farm lets recorded by indenture (see various indentures held in Bischoff papers, LBBLSA).

[12] Porter 1994, 131.

[13] *Ibid*, 134.

[14] Harvey 1970, 87.

[15] A copy is held in LBBLSA.

[16] Copies of both the Crow and Messeder maps are held in LBBLSA.

[17] Bischoff papers, B1/15 and 16, 1757, LBBLSA.

[18] Catalogue of Sale for the Parish Lands of Hendon, 1754/56, held in Barnet Archives. For the purpose of consistency the family name of Thomas Nicholl or Nicoll of Church End Farm is given in the text as Nicholl except where a direct quote from documentary material is given, when the written variant is provided.

[19] The 1763 sale is given by Ted Sammes as Registered in Middlesex, 7th May 1763, B2 No 345. Enrolled in the King's Bench Easter Term 3, George III, 1763, Roll No. 88.

[20] The land is described as fronting eastward on 'ground then in the possession of Nicholl', northward 'the garden ground then in the possession of William Dalmer Esq.', fronting west 'in part on a barn of Nicholl' and 'in other part on lands also then in the occupation of the said Nicoll.' (The spelling of Nicholl here is again variant.)

[21] LBBLSA, Print ref L6096. The approximate date is that given in the LBBLSA card index record. Coincidentally a letter from Rev. Denis Bayley, a great great great grandson of Thomas Nicholl, to Ted Sammes, dated 18 September 1963, records that William Bayley, son of Nancy Bayley, née Nicholl, and Thomas Nicholl's granddaughter, was an amateur artist of some ability. The Rev. Bayley then had '5 or 6 clever water-colours of Hendon scenes, c 1825–1830' in his possession. Letter held with the Church End Farm papers, Ted Sammes archive.

[22] Bischoff papers, B1/25.

[23] Prepared to accompany Cook's map, which is numerically referenced to the Field Book. Copies are held by LBBLSA.

[24] A Particular and Valuation of the Manor of Hendon in the County of Middlesex taken by Thomas Browne in March 1753. Micro film held at LBBLSA obtained by Middlesex Record Office from original now held at the National Library of Wales.

[25] Note Lloyd 1925, 46.

[26] By an Act of Geo. II (1730) responsibility for the prevention of certain abuses in the making of tiles and bricks and in prevention of unlawful combinations by tradesmen was passed to the Justices of the Peace (note Lloyd 1925, 49, 51).

[27] Note Lloyd 1925, 46.

[28] The Tylers' and Bricklayers' Company records are held at the Guildhall, in the City of London.

[29] Freedom Register of The Tylers' and Bricklayers' Company, Guildhall Library, 3053/3.

[30] Note Webb 1996, abstract of Ms 3045/2 Guildhall Library, page vi, on both the entry and practice of 'turning over'. A large number of apprentices, especially in the early 1700s, were apprenticed to one master 'to the intent that they be turned over' to another. Normally the master to whom the apprentice was turned over was not a member of the Tylers' and Bricklayers' Company, but was a bricklayer by trade.

[31] These details are taken from *Sources for tracing apprenticeship and membership in City Livery Companies and related organisations at Guildhall Library*, Guildhall Library 2005.

[32] See Lloyd 1925, 19 on the usual need to pay rent to a proprietor in digging brickearth.

[33] *Ibid*, 25, citing Batty Langley, *London Prices*, 1749, 85, 89, 94, 97.

[34] *Ibid*, 23–25, citing S Primatt, *The City and Country Purchaser and Builder* (2nd Edn by W Leybourne, 1680), and Batty Langley, *London Prices*, 1749.

[35] *Ibid*, 25, again citing Batty Langley, 1749.

[36] For an insight into the role (and potential tribulations) of journeymen bricklayers in the early and mid 18th century see Summerson 1970, 78.

[37] Pigot and Co's Directory for Middlesex and the Towns and Villages within 12 Miles of London, 450, entry for Hendon Parish. A copy is held at LBBLSA.

[38] *Op cit*, note 18; copy held at LBBLSA. This makes a distinction between meadow and arable under the heading 'Quality of the Lands'.

[39] *Op cit*, note 8.

[40] Notation by Ted Sammes within the archive from the Abstract of the Title of Walter Lyulph Johnson to freehold land at Hendon, Middx., prepared in 1927. This provides a description of Church End Farm identifying Church End House, Church End Farm farmhouse, and listing associated buildings, field use and acreages.

[41] Catalogue of Sale, and indenture dated 28 September 1874 (Hancock to Dunlop) transcribed by Ted Sammes. The indenture refers to land known as

Church End Farm, but which can be identified with confidence as Coles Farm (so named in a Catalogue of Sale longhand annotation) from a comparison of the field names.

[42] Details contained in a document presented on the death of a Mrs Lemon of Church Farm and held in a compilation for Church Farm, LBBLSA, ref. 728.67.

[43] Victoria County History, Vol. 5, 23.

[44] *Ibid*, 23.

[45] See No. 85, within 'Reference to Page 6', Field Book to Cook's Map, LBBLSA.

[46] The Book of Reference to the New Map of the Whole Manor and Parish of Hendon, in the County of Middlesex, Francis Whishaw, 1828, 20 gives for Church End Farm the description 'The Farm House, Barns, Garden and small Pightle', the latter meaning 'A small field or enclosure' (*The New Shorter Oxford English Dictionary*, 1993).

[47] Victoria County History, Vol. 5, 23, citing M. Rees, 'Extra-Metropolitan Middlesex', (London Univ. M.Sc. thesis, 1953), and St. Barts. Hosp., Hc 9/4.

[48] Bischoff papers, LBBLSA, B1/33. An Edward Nicoll is referred to in a schedule of deeds also held with the Bischoff papers (B1/137), which lists a licence of March 1812 to B J Johnson to demise land, and possibly Church End Farm, to a person of this name. The document referred to does not now seem to be held with the present Bischoff papers and may be lost. In 1815 an Edward Nicholl Jnr. is facilitating the removal of gravel from one of B J Johnson's fields and possibly, from the description, at Church End Farm (Bischoff papers, LBBLSA, B1/135). It may be safe to assume that he was holding the farm lease of Church End Farm in February 1815, and possibly as early as 1812. After taking a lease for the farm in April 1824, within a short time he is identified as a Bankrupt. Edward Nicholl the younger is described in 1827 (after bankruptcy) as hay salesman, dealer and chapman.

[49] Bischoff, B1/33.

[50] Bischoff, B1/39.

[51] See Woodforde 1983, 29; for the wider economic trends of the so-called Great Depression of the last quarter of the 19th century see, for example, Saul 1969. His Table 1, *Board of Trade Wholesale Price Indices (1871–5 = 100)*, covering the period 1871–1895, shows a decline in the index for animal products (including meat and dairy products) to an index of 84.6 for 1891–5, but for grains, a more dramatic decline for the corresponding index to 66.0.

[52] There is some evidence for multiple occupation of Church End Farm in 1841 (perhaps for both farm workers and artisan 'use') from the national census record.

[53] Bischoff, B/126, LBBLSA.

[54] See Bischoff, B1/137 referencing surrender Mr E. Wiggins to W. F. Johnson dated 11 April 1851, and, for later lease forms, see Bischoff, B1/46 and 47.

[55] LBBLSA collection for the Sweetland family.

[56] Sources consulted on micro film at LBBLSA: national census entries for Church End Farm 1881 and 1891, and Hendon Rate Books for 1882, 1885, 1886, 1887, 1888, 1889.

[57] 27 July 1927 Abstract of the Title of Walter Lyulph Johnson held in the LBBLSA collection, 10831/14. This suggests continued hay production.

[58] Ted Sammes' notation 'Conveyance of an Estate called (sic) Church End Farm situate in Hendon in the County of Middx. Dated 14 January 1873. Registered B2 No 933'. Ted Sammes Archive.

[59] The farm buildings south of Hall lane included a farmhouse 'now converted or used as two cottages', a labourer's cottage, barns, stables, garden and yard. The farmhouse seems to have survived as numbers 1, 2 and 3 Vine Cottages until the spring of 1935, but most of the rest was swept away on construction of the Model Dairy Farm. John Linnell's watercolour of September 1881 shows the large barn (probably early to mid 18th century) with the farmhouse beyond, with the rooflines of some of Church End Farm's buildings glimpsed in the right background.

[60] Ted Sammes Archive.

[61] LBBLSA MHS 2/119. Downey states that Andrew Dunlop 'farmed a fair number of acres northward from the parish church, …'. This suggests that the land below Hall Lane, including the Model Dairy Farm, was by then managed by others. The recollection continues 'Opposite Dunlop's was Hinge's Farm. Jim Hinge and his brother Will did well here for a great many years, and Miss Nellie Hinge carries on the good work today.'

[62] Copy of a letter held in a compilation for Church

Farm, LBBLSA.

⁶³ From an obituary notice for Mrs Hinge in the Hendon and Finchley Times for 17 July 1914 (LBBLSA collection for the Hinge family).

⁶⁴ From a compilation for Church End Farm, LBBLSA. James Henry Hinge's occupation is given as dairy farmer in the Official Search documentation, date-stamped 8th June 1942, also held by LBBLSA.

⁶⁵ LBBLSA architectural drawing reproduced in 'Building News' for 19th July 1889 as Print L3393. Cherry and Pevsner (1998, 163), however, give the buildings as of 1889 by W*imperis and Arbour* for C F Hancock of Hendon Hall, noting the chief survival as the long milking parlour at right angles to the road with its apsed-shaped hay loft and finial.

⁶⁶ Further leases, W L Johnson to John (*sic*?) Henry Hinge and William Hinge, dated 3rd January 1921 for ten years from 29th September 1916 and dated 29th November 1926 for 11 months from 29th September 1926, are recorded in the 27th July 1927 Abstract of the Title of Walter Lyulph Johnson held in the LBBLSA collection. The rental is now only £140 per annum. This may reflect land sales and lease grants over time to the Midland Railway, Graham White and others, recorded in the Abstract.

⁶⁷ Middlesex Deeds Official Search Reference. No 3895/39, LBBLSA.

⁶⁸ See, for example, details of a disposal of Miss Hinge's land, Hendon, in the vicinity of the Barnet Bypass, 1929, LBBLSA 10831/23.

⁶⁹ Item in Hendon and Finchley Times for 7th December 1957, LBBLSA. Miss Hinge is reported here as having won a Middlesex silver challenge cup for her small herd of cows.

⁷⁰ Louis Wulff, in a Property and Planning newspaper feature, held in LBBLSA collection for Church End Farm.

⁷¹ Clive Smith, of Memories, Brent Street, Hendon (then of Fuller Street) recalls helping out his Uncle Bert (only eight years his senior and still a teenager) with work on the farm soon after the 1939–45 war. He remembers the cattle from this time, as well as the pigs, allowed in the early 1960s to roam in The Paddock during the day.

⁷² F W H Abrams, Transactions No. 2 (New Series), of the Mill Hill and Hendon Historical Society on the Kempes of Hendon and Church Farm House, 4. Copy in LBBLSA.

⁷³ See Harvey 1970, 72.

⁷⁴ *Ibid*, 72.

⁷⁵ *Ibid*, 72.

⁷⁶ 'Estate' is perhaps a little grand for a holding of some 115 acres, but it is the term used on the Rankin and Johnson plan of 1789.

⁷⁷ There is possible evidence for multiple occupation of Church End Farm in 1841 (and perhaps both farm and artisan 'use') from the national census record.

⁷⁸ Braun 1962, 73, 75; Addy (revised Summerson) 1975, 73-4. Braun 1962, 75-76, in discussing measurement of the vernacular farmhouse cites one basic unit as the span of the building, probably from 16 to 20 feet across, the other as the bay unit, 'possibly twelve feet but perhaps as much as sixteen'. See also his other remarks on metrology on pages 25-6, *ibid*. In terms of plan forms, as given by Brunskill (2000, 108-9), the original Church End Farm would conform to the central fireplaces family. ' Addy's description (77), of a house of this general character at Upper Midhope, near Penistone, is admirable for conjuring an image of the access to the upper rooms, including in this case an oak hand rail to the stair, but noting also the use elsewhere of a rope for the same purpose. Such a rope could be found in use at Oxgate Farm, Coles Green Road, Brent, a timber-framed house of 16th- and 17th-century date, with a south range conforming to the lobby-entrance plan.

⁷⁹ Terry Smith pers. comm. Besides the pre-destruction photography, we have no evidence for the type of roof structure at Church End Farm, although in the south-east and east of England the early vernacular form of crown-post construction did not utilise ridge poles. See Brown 1982, 174–79.

⁸⁰ Machine-cut weatherboarding might tend to suggest a 19th century or later date. Compare the weatherboarding in the Church End Farm photograph with four examples of extant weatherboarding (1919 or earlier) on small Georgian houses shown in Ramsey and Harvey 1972, plates 46, 47 and 48.

⁸¹ See Lynch 1994, 42 and Cave 1981, 121.

[82] Malcolm Airs, 'Timber-framed buildings' in the Introduction to Cherry and Pevsner 1991, 103-104.

[83] *Ibid*, 104.

[84] *Ibid*, 104.

[85] Braun 1962, 75-76.

[86] *Ibid*, 85.

[87] *Ibid*, 85.

[88] *Ibid*, 25.

[89] LBBLSA L3091.

[90] Braun 1962, 25-26.

[91] Gerrard Roots, pers. comm.. See also Cherry and Pevsner (1998, 63), where a plan of Church Farm farmhouse is given, with proposed generalised building dates for surviving elements. The description notes 'Chiefly C17, with red brick three-

bay front of two storeys divided by a plat band; three widely spaced gables with original dormer windows… . Fine grouped chimneystack with four flues, between parlour (l.) and hall (r.). Kitchen to the r. of the hall, with large rear fireplace.' (*Ibid.*, 164).

[92] Lynch (1994, 43) notes that English bond or English cross bond remained popular throughout the Stuart period. Most sources seem to suggest that it was becoming rare by the early 18th century.

[93] *Ibid*, 86.

[94] A type given by Brunskill (2000, 145) as typical of the late 18th century.

[95] Some reliance is placed here on the limited view provided by the Thomas Bailey watercolour of the north range of the yard, and the inference drawn from the 1863 OS mapping concerning timber structures at the west end of Hinge's Yard.

[96] See note 21 above.

[97] Bischoff, B1/108 and 116, 1892, overlaid on 1863 OS mapping.

[98] A Particular and Valuation of the Manor of Hendon in the County of Middlesex, *op cit*.

[99] The watercolour is now in a private collection, and is reproduced here by kind permission. The painting is likely to have been made by John Linnell Jnr. The famous John Linnell Snr died in January 1882 at the age of 89, and had ceased to paint some time before his death.

[100] Brunskill 1987, 40.

[101] *Ibid*, 42.

[102] See Peters 1981, 16; Brunskill 1987, 41, 114-15.

[103] A lancet window is a narrow window with an arched top. The two narrow windows in the slideare shown at an oblique angle and could be round-headed, although it seemed fair enough to give them the architectural aspiration they appear to reflect.

[104] A note prepared in the autumn of 1965 for a display screen for the exhibition of finds from Church End Farm 1961 –65, held at Church Farm House Museum from September to November 1965 has survived in the archive. The display screen included drawings and plans of the barn by A R Leeds. The display screen note records that '… an examination of the timbers of the barn shows that a quantity of charred wood has been re-used in the present building', linking this to Thomas Browne's 1753 report of a barn fire at Church End Farm in the early 1750s. The note also records that the rear of the barn could be seen from 'the windows of the museum'. It concludes with the following assessment of its importance as a standing building: 'The barn as it stands today is important because it is one of the very few remaining barns of its type left in Middlesex; a similar building on Coldharbour Farm, Hayes, Middlesex, with the date 1806 on the tie beam has recently been demolished. It was decided therefore that as accurate as possible a record should be made of the barn'.

[105] Finds now held in Barnet Museum.

[106] Pearce 1992.

[107] Hurst *et al* 1986, 66.

[108] *Ibid*, 102–104.

[109] Garner and Archer 1972, pl 43.

[110] See Korf 1981, figs 672–76 and 689–90.

[111] Hurst *et al* 1986, col. pl. III.

[112] *Ibid*, 242–51.

[113] For example, at Guildhall Yard East (MoL site code GYE92) and in Southwark, St Thomas' Street (STS82).

[114] Pearce 1992, 27–29.

[115] Gaimster 1997, fig 2.10.

[116] *Ibid*, no.50.

[117] *Ibid*, no. 53.

[118] Hughes 2003, 1.

[119] Analysis was carried out by Dr J N Walsh at the Department of Geology, Royal Holloway, University of London.

[120] Permission to reproduce this image was kindly given by Andrea Cameron, of the Hogarth House Museum, Chiswick.

[121] Bridge House Accounts, weekly payments, 2nd series, volume 2, 1516-1528 folio 377r (Corporation of London Records Office).

[122] Quoted by Christianson 2002.

[123] Rennie 1883, 485.

[124] Loudon 1842. 266.

[125] Clark 2000, 16.

[126] Barnard 1948.

[127] Brears 1974, 104.

[128] Notes and Queries 1881, 109.

[129] Clark 2000, 16.

[130] Evans 1970, 214.

[131] Summers-Smith 1963, 217.

[132] Site code MED90; Barber and Thomas 2002, 84.

[133] *Ibid*, 92.

[134] Divers 2004, 32.

[135] Ayto 1979, 4.

[136] De L'Ecluse, *Exoticorum Libri Decem*, of the 1540s, cited by Oswald 1975, 4.

[137] Identified by Adrian Oswald. See also Oswald 1975, 148.

[138] Ayto 1979, 6.

[139] Oswald 1975, 135.

[140] Atkinson 1975, 41.

[141] *Ibid*, 43.

[142] *Ibid*, 15.

[143] Ayto 1979, 6.

[144] *Ibid*, 10.

[145] Atkinson and Oswald 1969, fig 13.

[146] See Noel Hume 1969, 72, nos 12–14.

[147] Noel Hume 1961, 109.

[148] McIntyre 1973, 1.

[149] *Ibid*.

[150] Terry Smith pers. comm..

[151] We are most grateful to Dr Ian Betts, Museum of London Specialist Services, for identifying these tiles and supplying the descriptions given here.

[152] There are complete tiles, with the same design, in the Museum of London Ceramics and Glass Collection (eg A13155, P623). Pluis (1997, 212) illustrates a Dutch version of this design (no. A.01.03.54).

[153] For a complete example, see Horne 1989, 62, no 341.

[154] Jones 1995, 10.

[155] Atterbury and Batkin, 1999.

[156] Identification kindly provided by Miranda Goodby, Collections Officer at The Potteries Museum and Art Gallery, Stoke-on-Trent. See examples illustrated by Van Lemmen 2000, 29.

[157] Miranda Goodby, pers. comm.

[158] All coins and tokens were kindly identified by Dr Geoff Egan, Museum of London Specialist Services.

[159] Geoff Egan pers. comm.

[160] Noel Hume 1969, 174–75.

[161] Geoff Egan pers. comm.

[162] Objects identified by Geoff Egan.

[163] Geoff Egan, pers. comm.

[164] Identified by Andrew Coulson.

[165] Armitage 1978.

[166] Serjeantson 1986.

[167] Legge 1981.

[168] Serjeantson 1986.

[169] A J Legge, pers. comm.

[170] A J Legge, pers. comm.

[171] Serjeantson *et al* 1986.

[172] A J Legge pers. comm.

[173] Binford 1978.

[174] In refining further the idea of use, Binford (1978) went on to develop a general utility index (GUI) into which the Church End Farm animal bones have been fitted.

[175] This pattern accords with the criteria suggested by Serjeantson and Waldron (1989, 3) for recognising the bone waste from food use.

[176] Cohen and Serjeantson 1996.

[177] Coy 1989.

[178] Serjeantson 1989; A J Legge pers. comm.

[179] See Payne 1972a.

[180] Armitage 1984.

[181] Lawrence and Brown 1973.

[182] *Ibid.*

[183] J J Davies, ICAZ Animal Paleopathology Working Group, pers. comm.

[184] Hillson 1986.